EPHESIANS

Paul Gardner

EPHESIANS

Grace and Joy in Christ

Marisa,
It's a joy to welcome you
into membership at CCP. May The
Word of Christ dwell in you richly,

In Christ,

Paul Gardner

Easter 2016

CHRISTIAN
FOCUS

Dr Paul Gardner was previously a lecturer in New Testament at Oak Hill Theological College in London and a Rural Dean in the Church of England. After serving as Archdeacon of Exeter for three years, in 2005 Dr. Gardner moved to Atlanta in the United States and now serves as the Senior Minister at ChristChurch Presbyterian, Atlanta.

Unless otherwise indicated scripture quotations are taken from *the Holy Bible, New International Version*. Copyright © 1973, 1978, 1984 by International Bible Society. Used by permission of Hodder & Stoughton Publishers, A member of the Hodder Headline Group. All rights reserved. 'NIV' is a registered trademark of International Bible Society. UK trademark number 1448790.

In Christ Alone by Keith Getty & Stuart Townend administered by worshiptogether.com songs excluding UK & Europe, administered by kingswaysongs.com. email: tym@kingsway.co.uk

ISBN 1-84550-264-7
ISBN 978-1-84550-264-5

© Paul Gardner

10 9 8 7 6 5 4 3 2 1

Published in 2007
in the
Focus on the Bible Commentary series
by
Christian Focus Publications, Ltd.,
Geanies House, Fearn, Ross-shire,
IV20 1TW, Great Britain.

www.christianfocus.com

Edited by Malcolm Maclean

Cover design by Danie Van Straaten

Printed by CPD Wales

Contents

Introduction

The epistle to the Ephesians is surely one of the most powerful in the New Testament. It is profoundly Trinitarian in its emphases. The letter speaks of God's sovereign plan and purposes to call into being a people who would exist for his praise and glory and who would be holy and blameless before him. It speaks of the grace and love of Christ in drawing a people to himself through his sacrificial death on the cross and his subsequent exaltation. Then the letter also speaks of the Spirit's work in guaranteeing the promised blessings for God's people, and of his empowering and infilling of them so they can live the holy lives to which they are called and work in unity as the church of God.

Commentators have often debated two key issues in this letter. The first concerns the main theme or purpose of the letter and the second concerns the authorship. While we cannot possibly do justice to all that has been said on these important matters, they deserve a few comments here.

Purpose of Ephesians: Encouragement and joy in Christ
Ephesians contains deep descriptions of God's purposes for his church. It describes the joy and encouragement to be found 'in Christ'. It provides instructions for living as Christians in a pagan environment, and it even portrays the writer's prayers for the people he addresses. The letter also addresses the matter of unity in the church and the need for mutual submission, for prayer, and for a bold proclamation of the gospel. So wide is the compass of what is addressed in these few pages that it is not possible to see one particular issue or problem giving rise to its being sent. Equally, although some have attempted to put all its teaching under one heading and one overarching theme, this may seem too restrictive.

However, in the last few verses we see that the writer has
sent the letter with Tychicus so that Tychicus may encourage
these Christians who have been concerned to hear of Paul's
imprisonment. If we look back through this letter, we can
see how the whole letter in fact seems to be concerned with
providing this sense of encouragement. Therefore, a summary
statement that we might keep in mind in reading the book, if
one is needed, is simply this: *Encouragement and joy in Christ.*

The letter starts with a listing of the extraordinary privileges,
the inheritance, that God's people have 'in Christ'. The phrase
is repeated again and again in the first chapter. This provides
the background against which life must be lived, for God
has already 'seated us [Christians] with him in the heavenly
places in Christ Jesus' (2:6). This should be a deep source of
encouragement in many ways to all Christians, but not least to
those who are concerned for the apostle who is languishing in
prison. One of the reasons he is in prison is precisely because
it has been part of his calling to bring the gospel to Gentiles.
In the gospel we find they too, if they receive it in faith, are 'in
Christ' and receive all the blessings that have been promised
to God's people. Thus the church finds its unity in Christ and
must be encouraged to seek and develop that unity. Likewise,
those who are in Christ are to be distinguished by the way
they live. They 'are light in the Lord' (5:8) and their behaviour
should reflect the fact that they are 'created after the likeness
of God in true righteousness and holiness' (4:24). The strength
to live as they should, to stand for the gospel, and to proclaim
the gospel boldly is to be found 'in the Lord and in the strength
of his might' (6:10).

For the writer there is extraordinary joy and encouragement
to be found, even while in prison, in knowing that God's
people are 'in Christ'. There we find where our true treasure
is, there we find we belong while in an alien world, there
we find strength to live for him, there we find unity among
believers as we enjoy God's church. Certainly as we read this
letter, we should be encouraged. Many wonderful theological
truths are addressed, many challenges are laid before God's
people but, in the end, one truth shines out for which we are

to praise God: 'he has blessed us in the heavenly realms with every spiritual blessing in Christ' (1:3).

Authorship

This commentary takes the position that the apostle Paul wrote this letter. However, the debates over authorship are very extensive indeed.[1] Those who speak against authorship by the apostle Paul give many different reasons for their position. Several reasons stand out. For example, it is said that some of the doctrine presented in Ephesians is not found elsewhere in Paul, especially some of the teaching about the church. It is also suggested that the Greek style seems different from other letters by Paul, for example, sentence length is greater in Ephesians and some vocabulary is used here that is not found in others of Paul's letters. Others make certain assumptions based on the similarities between Ephesians and Colossians. They say that the same writer would hardly have written both letters around the same time, and so Ephesians is probably later and that the writer uses some of Paul's theological ideas and words from Colossians. Some argue that the letter is too impersonal for Paul to have written it to a city which he had known well.

The defence of apostolic authorship is only needed when it is challenged. The book claims to be by the apostle Paul and it is almost certainly attested to earlier than any other New Testament book. It seems very likely that Clement of Rome, writing at the turn of the first century in his first epistle to the Corinthians, alludes to it in several places. Other very early leaders of the church, such as Ignatius, refer to verses from this epistle, and Polycarp (69–135), bishop of Smyrna, actually quotes Ephesians 4:26 and refers to it as Scripture. Irenaeus talks of Ephesians as being written by Paul. In fact there are numerous early sources (within the first 100–125 years of its writing) that state Ephesians was written by Paul.

---

1 The format of this commentary series precludes such detailed examination of these preliminary issues. Two more recent extensive commentaries which have argued for Pauline authorship may be of interest. Both interact in detail with those who would take an alternative position. P. T. O'Brien, *The Letter to the Ephesians* (Leicester: Apollos, 1999), and H.W. Hoehner, *Ephesians. An Exegetical Commentary* (Grand Rapids: Baker, 2002).

Linguistic differences are always difficult to assess. The fact of the matter is that Paul is an excellent writer, and can change his style even within those undisputed Pauline epistles. He also used a scribe from time to time, and even then we actually do not have a great deal of literature by him with which to compare styles in the first place!

The lack of personal references in a letter supposedly written to a church where Paul had lived for a lengthy period of time may well be explained by the fact that the letter was probably for a wider circulation among a number of other churches in Asia Minor. The specific designation 'In Ephesus' in verse 1 is not attested to by the earliest manuscripts but, anyway, may have referred to the largest of a number of churches to whom the letter was being carried. Nevertheless, there are many personal additions to this letter which would speak against pseudonymity. For example, the author knows of the 'faith' and the 'love for all the saints' for which this church is noted (1:15). He asks for prayers for himself (6:19). He knows these people have a very special concern for him as he sits in prison, which also suggests that he had a special relationship with them, even to the extent that he sends a friend to reassure them about his welfare (6:21ff). ·

Many of the great theological themes so obvious in the undisputed epistles of Paul are in fact present here very clearly. For example, the centrality of grace, the description of justification by faith, the work of Christ in reconciliation and the drawing together of Jew and Gentile, the description of those who are not Christ's and those who are, and even the use of the phrase we talked of earlier, 'in Christ', which is so much part of Paul's theology in, say, Romans, 1 Corinthians and Galatians.

From our point of view, we may also add that Scripture must be allowed to be Scripture. Arguments that suggest it is possible both to hold to the trustworthiness of God's Word and believe in pseudonymity are novel but, in the end, unpersuasive. All manuscripts attest to Paul's authorship in verse 1, very early writers all seem to accept his authorship and here we proceed on this basis.

Date of Ephesians
It is most likely that this letter was written from Rome, sometime in the period of AD 60–62. We know Paul was in prison when he wrote (3:1, 4:1, 6:20). While he had been imprisoned in Caesarea two or three years earlier, it seems that the Roman imprisonment, described in Acts 28, fits the facts better. The imprisonment in Rome was something akin to 'house arrest', and visitors like Tychicus or Timothy could come and go with reports for the churches of how Paul was coping, taking his epistles to the churches, and returning with news of how they were progressing. Acts 28:20 tells us that Paul was chained during this imprisonment, a detail also mentioned by Paul in 6:20. If this view is correct, and it is certainly held by the majority of commentators, then we may trace Paul's journey to this point as recorded in Acts 21ff.

Paul travelled from Caesarea, where he met up with Philip and his daughters (Acts 21:8-14) and was warned not to go to Jerusalem. However, Paul did travel to Jerusalem where he was received 'gladly' and met up with James and the elders (v. 17 ff). After the crowds were organised against the apostle, he was arrested. He was allowed to address the crowds and gave his testimony (Acts 22). It was at the point of mentioning his call to the Gentiles (22:21) that the crowd rioted and Paul's arrest was confirmed. The Jews planned to kill him (23:12), but the plot was discovered and Paul was taken to Felix. He was then taken to Rome (Acts 27) where he was imprisoned and from there it seems most likely he wrote this epistle, Colossians, Philemon and Philippians.

The Church at Ephesus
We read of the Church at Ephesus in Acts 18. The apostle Paul had been working in Corinth for some time and then moved on to Ephesus where he left Priscilla and Aquila (Acts 18:19). As was Paul's habit on entering a new town, he went into the synagogue to talk to the Jews first. It appears that he was warmly received, at least for a while. However, he needed to get back to Antioch and so refused a request to stay on at Ephesus (18:20-22). In 18:24-28, there is an interesting aside about the development of the church in this city. Apollos, who

was a great teacher and well taught in the Scriptures, came to speak to the Jews. He clearly knew something of the Lord, but was taken aside by Priscilla and Aquila and taught the Christian faith more deeply. He was renowned for refuting the Jews in public debate and 'proving from the Scriptures that Jesus was the Christ' (v. 28). In Acts 19 Paul returned to Ephesus where he baptized some disciples 'into the name of the Lord Jesus'. These disciples appear to have been faithful Jews who were awaiting the coming of Christ, having been baptized under John the Baptist's ministry. Paul once again entered the synagogue where he spoke 'boldly for three months'. As so often happened, Paul was eventually forced out of the synagogue by some who refused to believe and so he moved to the lecture hall of Tyrannus. There he preached the gospel to Jew and Gentile alike. Specifically we are told in 19:10 that Paul was able to address people from the whole 'province of Asia'. Paul performed great miracles in the city and a great many people came to faith.

Magic and the gods at Ephesus
As in all the cities of the Roman Empire, many gods were worshipped in Ephesus, including Caesar himself. However, it was the goddess Artemis who dominated the city's religious affairs. People would travel from different parts of the empire to worship at her temple. So great was the cult of Artemis that local tradesmen made their living from selling silver shrines and images of her. It was this that, in the end, forced Paul to have to leave the city. The tradesmen rioted against him and his message. In 19:26 we see that it is Paul's attack on 'man-made gods' that incurs the anger of the townspeople. It is one thing for Christ to be preached as one of many choices of gods, but it is altogether another thing when the apostle preaches the truth that there is only one God.

Ephesus was also noted for its commitment to the practice of magic. One of the evidences of changed lives in the hearts of the new believers was that they came and 'openly confessed their evil deeds' (v. 18). Those who practised magic brought numerous, very valuable scrolls to be burned. The result of this was that 'the word of the Lord spread widely and grew in power'.

Given this background, it is not surprising that the Apostle Paul emphasises, as he writes this letter to the Ephesians, that Christians have left the world of darkness and are now to be found 'in Christ'. He takes time to stress that, while the spiritual forces of evil are powerful, nevertheless Christians are safe 'in Christ' and are 'seated in the heavenly places' (Eph. 2:6). Lest the Ephesians feel that the cult of Artemis, or the practice of magic, or the power of other gods is overwhelming, Paul also emphasises the power that Christians have in the Lord (specially see 1:19-23; also 3:16; 3:18, 20; 6:10).

The Ephesian Elders
One further section of the account in Acts of Paul's work at Ephesus is worth mentioning here. In Acts 20:17 ff we read of Paul travelling via Miletus on his way to Jerusalem. From Miletus he sends word to the Ephesian elders asking them to come and see him. In his exhortation to the elders we learn something more about his ministry in the city. For example, he visited 'house to house'. He also mentions that he did not hesitate to preach anything that was necessary for the development of the Christian faith. In his exhortation the apostle urged the Ephesian elders to 'keep watch over' themselves and over the flock of which they were overseers (20:28). Paul was clearly afraid that this church will succumb to false teaching and to the 'savage wolves' who would seek to destroy the flock. He was concerned that, even from among the leaders, men would arise who would distort the truth and seek to draw people to follow them. Paul knew that he would not see these elders again (v. 25) and so he was urgent in his desire to ensure that they would uphold the truth and not succumb to any false teaching. No doubt, as he wrote his letter, he was concerned with similar matters. His emphasis on how they should live (Eph. 3–6), and on the power of God, and the need to follow the truth, all indicate his continuing concern for them.

Two Further Chapters In The Story
Sometime after Paul wrote the letter to the Ephesians, he wrote his first epistle to Timothy. This is of interest because

he asks Timothy to stay in Ephesus for a while and stop those leaders, who were already promoting 'false doctrines', from teaching. It seems that the apostle's early fears for the church, as expressed in Acts, had in some measure been realised.

Years after the letter to the Ephesians has been written and the apostle Paul had been martyred in Rome, the Apostle John was given a letter in a vision from the Lord Jesus Christ to this church at Ephesus. It is recorded for us in Revelation 2:1-7. It is interesting to reflect back on the epistle and on the account in Acts and see what has happened in a period of some 25 years or so. Jesus begins in Revelation 2:1-3 by encouraging the church. As Paul expected, they have endured many hardships, yet in spite of this, they have not grown weary. No doubt, following Paul's early concern for them and Timothy's later admonitions, Christ is able to comment favourably in this letter that they 'cannot tolerate wicked men'. They have 'tested' people as leaders and have found out those who were false. Not only that, but the Ephesian Christians continued to hate evil practices (v. 6). This suggests that they were continuing to confront the battle with magic and with the cult of Artemis. Certainly there is much in this letter to encourage this church that has survived its first quarter century reasonably well. However, Jesus does pick up on a problem. They have lost their 'first love' (2:4). What appears to have happened is that, in their constant battle against those who were attacking the faith and those who were seeking to lead them astray, their initial enthusiasm and desire to be missionaries to the world around them had dissipated. Jesus warns them that they should repent and go back to doing things in the way they did at the beginning of their church's life (v. 5). The church was clearly in danger of dying out simply because, though theologically orthodox, it had lost its missionary purpose. Christ's warning at the end of this letter is serious enough, but he also makes a promise to them that if they persevere they will indeed enjoy 'the paradise of God'.

Gospel People

(Ephesians 1–3)

1

Greetings from the apostle Paul
(Ephesians 1:1-2)

Paul, an apostle of Christ Jesus by the will of God, To the saints in Ephesus, the faithful in Christ Jesus: Grace and peace to you from God our Father and the Lord Jesus Christ (1:1-2).

Paul[1] begins this letter by drawing attention to his own calling and apostolic authority. He will discuss later the calling of those to whom he is writing, but his own was unique. He was called specifically by the voice of Jesus on the road to Damascus (Acts 9:3-9), and in Acts 26:15-18 he describes how, in that great episode in his life, he was specifically appointed by God as an apostle who was to reach out to the Gentiles[2] so that they might turn 'from darkness to light', a theme to which he will return in this letter (e.g. 5:8ff).

Paul writes to people who are **the saints**, that is, Christians. In today's English the word may imply people more 'holy' in their lives than is normal, but here Paul is referring specially to those who are set apart by God to be his people. It is a term that can be used of all Christian people and here it designates those who worship in the churches in Ephesus.[3] These people

---

1 The apostolic authorship is briefly examined in the Introduction.

2 He takes up again the matter of his calling to take the gospel to the Gentiles and refers back to the Damascus road in 3:1-13.

3 The words 'in Ephesus' are missing from a number of early manuscripts. It seems likely, if these words were added a little later, that Ephesus was the main city to which the letter was written. Perhaps the letter would have been passed on to other

are also said to be **the faithful**. In other words, they are people of faith, believers.

The next phrase, **in Christ Jesus**, is one of Paul's most loved expressions and means a lot more than simply 'being a Christian'. Being 'in Christ' or 'in Christ Jesus' pulls together all that is Christian existence. It sums up all that Christians have and are as 'co-heirs' (Rom. 8:17) with Christ, as his people. It speaks of the huge privileges that are ours, and the great inheritance that is ours. The phrase points to the fact that Christ is truly our representative King. He brings us before God and brings God to us. (We shall see in due course that in many ways what is true of our King can also be said to be true of us. For example, see on 2:5-6.) Being 'in Christ' is therefore an immense privilege for all who are called and have faith in him.

Both God the Father and the Lord Jesus Christ are the source of all **grace** and **peace** for believers. *Grace* describes God's amazing and unmerited love and mercy that he shows to all his people. It is experienced in conversion but then also in God's continuing help throughout life, which is what Paul has in mind here. *Peace* is both the peace with God in which those who are in Christ find they are no longer enemies of God but 'reconciled' to him (Rom. 5:10), and it is also the peace experienced by believers as they know Christ's continuing work in their lives day by day.

---

local churches. It is likely that there would have been several gatherings of Christians, several churches, in the city itself.

2

Praise for God's blessings in Christ
(Ephesians 1:3-14)

Praise be to the God and Father of our Lord Jesus Christ, who has blessed us in the heavenly realms with every spiritual blessing in Christ. For he chose us in him before the creation of the world to be holy and blameless in his sight. In love he predestined us to be adopted as his sons through Jesus Christ, in accordance with his pleasure and will – to the praise of his glorious grace, which he has freely given us in the One he loves. In him we have redemption through his blood, the forgiveness of sins, in accordance with the riches of God's grace that he lavished on us with all wisdom and understanding. And he made known to us the mystery of his will according to his good pleasure, which he purposed in Christ, to be put into effect when the times will have reached their fulfilment – to bring all things in heaven and on earth together under one head, even Christ. In whom we were also chosen, having been predestined according to the plan of him who works out everything in conformity with the purpose of his will, in order that we, who were the first to hope in Christ, might be for the praise of his glory. And you also were included in Christ when you heard the word of truth, the gospel of your salvation. Having believed, you were marked in him with a seal, the promised Holy Spirit, who is a deposit guaranteeing our inheritance until the redemption of those who are God's possession – to the praise of his glory (1:3-14).

It is difficult properly to convey these next twelve verses in English. In the Greek, verses 3-14 seem almost to bubble off Paul's tongue. He is thinking of the extraordinary grace and blessing that belongs to all who are 'in Christ', and as he does so his enthusiasm pours out in one long sentence of praise to God. (The NIV has inserted full stops at vv. 3, 4, 6, 9, 10 and 12 in order to make this more readable in English.) Perhaps it is worth reading this whole section really quickly without pausing at the stops in order to get a feeling of the joy and enthusiasm Paul experiences as he speaks of such wonderful truths.

Above all, what drives Paul forward in his praise is the thought that God, in his love and grace, should have planned a people who would stand before him and who would receive blessing upon blessing from him, and that all this has happened 'in Christ'. Paul's excitement as he thinks of all the blessings God has given us 'in Christ', is also emphasised as Paul repeats again and again the words 'in Christ' or 'in him' (11 times).

It is worth seeing this laid out below, a little more literally, in order better to understand the weight Paul is giving to the whole glorious concept of what it is for believers to find themselves 'in Christ'.

Praise to the God ... who has blessed us ... *in Christ* (v. 3).
he chose us *in him* (v. 4) to be holy ... in his sight
In love he predestined us (v. 5).
to be adopted as his sons *through Jesus Christ* ...
to the praise of his glorious grace, with which he has graced
　　us *in the One he loves* (v. 6).
In him we have redemption through his blood (v. 7) ...
He made known ... according to his will which he purposed
　　in him ... (v. 9).
to bring all things together *in Christ*, things in heaven and
　　on earth, *in him* (v. 10)
in whom (v. 11) we were also chosen ...
first to hope *in Christ* (v. 12)
in whom you also are, having heard the word of truth ...
　　(v. 13)
and *in whom*, having believed you were sealed with the
　　Holy Spirit (v 13) ...

a) Blessed by the Father in Christ (v. 3)

Paul's praise is of God whom he knows as the Father of our Lord Jesus Christ. This is of particular significance here because it is in and through the Lord Jesus Christ that God's will to bless his people has actually happened. And Paul says that God has blessed us. He is writing to those who believe and are therefore God's people, and he includes himself as he says 'us'. As we read, therefore, we too may include ourselves, if we have faith in Christ. Through this whole section Paul will talk of 'we' and 'us', because what he is saying is true of all who are 'in Christ'. The passage thus becomes one of enormous comfort and encouragement to us as Christians in the twenty-first century as it would have been to the Ephesian Christians. But more than that, it also therefore becomes a model passage for Christians as we think of all for which we too must give thanks and praise to God.

Christians have been blessed **in the heavenly realms ... in Christ**. Christ is situated at the right hand of the Father (1:20). As the one who has been raised from the dead and exalted to Lord over all, he is seated 'in the heavenly places' (2:6). This is a description of the place where Christ is enthroned and from which he and the Father rule. It describes a reality that is not always apparent to Christians in this age, which is that Christ is glorified (1:20) and has been exalted by the Father. This is the reality that will finally be shown to all people with the coming of the new heaven and the new earth, but the great news is that, though somewhat hidden, it already exists, and Christians are part of it (see on 2:6)! Of course, there is also a heavenly realm from which Satan and his forces attack (6:12) but, at this point, Paul is concerned about the blessings that we have 'in Christ'. Because we are 'in him' we find ourselves experiencing now the blessings of these heavenly realms.

As Christ represents his people, so it is as if they were there with Christ themselves. This is so vivid and real to Paul that in 2:6 he can talk of the Christian's present state as being 'seated with Christ in the heavenly realms **in Christ**'. The fact that these blessings are spiritual reminds us that all our blessings are in a true sense 'Trinitarian'. In Paul's writing the word 'spiritual' almost exclusively points to that which comes from or is used by the Holy Spirit, and these blessings are applied to the heart and life of the Christian and sealed for the Christian by the Holy Spirit (see v. 13 below). So Paul praises the Father for blessings mediated to us by the Holy Spirit that we have as Christians because we are 'in Christ'.

b) Chosen in Christ (v. 4)

We are now introduced to the great theme of God's election. The awesome electing action of God in salvation is the foundation of all the blessings that belong to Christians. Paul will spell out some of these, but the initial work of God in the election of his people in Christ is, for Paul, the overwhelming blessing. Here in verse 4 we find that God **chose us in Christ**. But this is added to in the verses which follow with talk of God's **will** and of how he **predestined us**. This great teaching reminds us that **every spiritual blessing in Christ** with which we have been blessed is entirely from God and comes to Christians by his grace. Significantly, these blessings are all of his purpose and plan. Just as Paul emphasised that it was by the **will** of God that he was called to be an apostle (v. 1), so now it is according to God's good **pleasure and will** (v. 5) that we are **predestined**. He will go on to discuss the *mystery* of God's will later. Meanwhile, as Paul continues his praise, he reflects on why and when God chose us, and how it all came about.

Though we can hardly begin to penetrate the mind of God, yet he has revealed some glorious things to us concerning his purposes and will. It is his will to have a people who will stand before him and be **holy** or 'set apart' to him, a people who will be wholly devoted to him and **blameless** (v. 4). Much of this was prefigured in the sacrificial lambs that had to be without blemish and were then devoted to God in sacrifice. It was God's will that such a people should have Christ as their King and representative, for this happens **in him**.

In the modern world we are often preoccupied with questions of 'success' or 'failure' in our lives. We wonder whether we have done enough for friends and neighbours, for employers and parents, but we are often tempted as well to ask whether we have done enough for God. It is, of course, right and proper to ask whether we are serving God as we should, but our place as 'saints', as 'holy ones' (v. 1), comes about because this is God's will and our holiness and blamelessness appear not because we are somehow struggling harder than others, or are more 'moral' people than others, but because all this happens *in him*. This is all about God's will and purpose in which he brings into being this people through **the grace which he has freely given us in the One he loves** (v. 6).

If we ask why God should want such a people, then verse 6 is as close as we come to an answer – **to the praise of his glorious grace**. God's ultimate aim is that he reveal his glory, that is, his nature and character. When this is revealed it always redounds to his praise. Paul knows that the predestining, saving work of God has as its goal that God will be glorified for who he is, and here we specially remember that part of God's character is that he is gracious. The idea, slightly modified, is also present in verses 11-12 where 'we' were 'chosen … in order that we … might be for the praise of his glory'. It is also the end product of our redemption, that we 'are God's own possession, to the praise of his glory' (v. 14).

In and through Christ, God calls into being a people that reflects something of the glory of God himself and thus brings praise to his glory. Thus God's aim is that, as his character is revealed in what he does for his people and in how they reflect that character, so his glory will truly be praised.

…before the creation [foundation] of the world (v. 4). In heaven God, in his wonderful plan for revealing his glory to his very great and eternal praise, planned to call into being a people set apart to him, and whose King would be Jesus. Seeing and knowing that we would fall into sin, he 'chose us in Christ'. We can hardly fathom the glory of this truth. In the mind of God, before even the foundation of this earth, God planned a people who would be devoted to him and reflect his image. That plan included the purpose to reveal his grace and love. God saw through the time when all would rebel and sin and turn against him, and before even the foundation of the world, he formed his plan to show his grace and love to us. Right back then he planned that 'in him', 'in Jesus' we would be chosen – in other words, that Jesus would indeed die on the cross and would do so for our sin, representing us. 'In Christ' we were chosen not just because it sounded like a nice idea, but because it was God's plan all along that there would be a people in the world who would be **holy and blameless in his sight.**

c) Adopted in Christ (v. 5)

The emphasis on God's electing grace and his plan and purpose from before creation comes through in verse after verse here. Verse 5 reminds us that 'love' is at the heart of this grace. **In love he predestined us to be adopted as his sons.** We shall see the significance of being his sons, shortly. But this family imagery helps remind us that the nature of God's love is not just an abstract concept. Rather God's love is revealed as he enters a relationship with his people. This relationship was also in accordance with his pleasure and will. Significantly the phrase 'in Christ' here is replaced by 'in the One he loves'. As Jesus is the beloved Son and in relationship with the Father so, in him, we find we too, in love, become adopted as his sons. What is true of Christ our King is true of us who are 'in him', represented and caught up in Christ before the Father: he is the Beloved, we are loved.

i) Sons and their inheritance

It is worth noting the significance that being called 'sons' carries with it. When Paul talks of us as 'sons', he is by no means excluding women. In fact, much the opposite. Paul can speak of God being a father to his 'sons and daughters' in 2 Corinthians 6:18 (quoting Isa. 43:6). But usually when using the word 'sons', Paul has in mind all that Christians inherit in Christ. In Paul's day sons would inherit from the father, while most daughters did not receive an independent inheritance. By saying that we are adopted as sons and relating this to all those who are in Christ, Paul is saying that all men and women (contrary to the norm of Paul's day), and even slaves, are equal members of this family. For a woman or slave as much as for a man, being 'in Christ' means that what is true for the King is true for his people. Christ is the Son who has come into and will come into his inheritance, and we, believing men and women, are adopted sons who also have come into and will come into a guaranteed inheritance (v. 14).

But sonship also implies a family resemblance. In his love for us in Christ, God adopted us to be part of his family. This means we will bear a resemblance to Christ as we live for him. Paul's joy at the thought of this great family, and the fact that all of this has been part of God's great will and purpose for his glory, gives rise to a lovely play on words here which is missed in some versions. He says in verse 6: 'to the praise of the glory of his *grace*, with which he has *graced* us in the One who is loved.'

ii) The depth of God's love for his children
As we study what Paul means by this phrase 'in Christ', one thing becomes clear again and again. What God does in Christ for us is the perfect and full expression of God's love for us. To be 'in Christ' is undoubtedly to experience the great depths of God's love for us. So extraordinary was the depth of this love that God would reveal to his praise and glory that, even before the world was founded, God was thinking and planning its demonstration in the lives of us who are sinners. This is to the glory of God who has so generously and freely lavished on us (v. 8) his grace in the Beloved, in Christ.

Our position among this people and 'in Christ' happens through Jesus Christ, and this is in accordance with God's will (v. 5). That is, it was God's plan that Jesus should also be the means to our becoming a holy and blameless people in God's sight. In order to be holy before him and adopted as sons our sin and guilt must be dealt with. Jesus achieves this for us in his life and death and resurrection. It is not simply that Jesus *represents* us before the Father, but that he has in fact dealt with sin and gained forgiveness for all those whom he represents before the Father. This is not some 'legal fiction' that, as it were, pretends we are alright before God when really we are not. Rather, Christ truly represents a people whom he presents to the Father as holy and blameless because he really has paid the penalty for their sin, and gained their forgiveness. At the heart of this achievement by Christ on behalf of his people is Christ's redeeming death.

Paul knows that only those who are redeemed and for-given will ever make up part of this people. Thus he refers in shorthand to the great sacrifice of Christ on the cross. He does this with two summary words, **redemption** and **blood**.

d) Redeemed in Christ (vv. 7-8)

Redemption has in mind the Old Testament background of Israel being redeemed or freed from slavery in Egypt. Deuteronomy 7:6-8 is significant for much of Paul's argument here in verses 4, 5 and 7. In Deuteronomy Moses had rejoiced in the way God had chosen Israel. Just as Paul here has given reasons for election that are to be found in the character of God, in his grace and love, so Moses had done the same.

> The LORD your God has chosen you out of all the peoples on the face of the earth to be his people, his treasured possession. The LORD did not set his affection on you and choose you because you were more numerous than other peoples, for you were the fewest of all peoples. But it was because the LORD loved you and kept the oath he swore to your forefathers that he brought you out with a mighty hand and redeemed you from the land of slavery, from the power of Pharaoh king of Egypt (Deut. 7:6b-8).

Israel came into existence by the plan and electing choice of God. As Paul has shown that this is born of God's love and grace, so Moses had stressed the same point. God has chosen them (Deut. 7:6, compare Eph. 1:4) because he loved them (Deut. 7:8, compare end Eph. 1:4, 'in love'). He did this by redeeming them from the land of slavery.

i) Freedom from slavery

In the New Testament Christ comes to fulfil all the Old Testament, not just specific promises, but to fulfil all that was being pointed to in the Old Testament Scripture. As Moses was God to Pharaoh (Exod. 7:1) in dealing with this king who put himself up against the King of kings, as the Lord redeemed the people of God out of death and slavery to freedom in the Exodus, so Christ deals with Satan (see Eph. 2:2) and leads those who are his into freedom, redeeming them from slavery (Gal. 5:1).

ii) Transfer from one kingdom to another

Redemption thus clearly implies a transfer of lordships, the removal from one kingdom to another. In Ephesians 5 Paul describes in more detail the contrast between what are the things of Christ's lordship, his kingdom, and the things that are of the kingdom of darkness (specially see 5:5). This link between redemption, the death of Christ, forgiveness and transfer of lordships is more explicit in Colossians 1:13-14: 'For he has rescued us from the dominion of darkness and brought us into the kingdom of the Son he loves, in whom we have redemption, the forgiveness of sins.'

iii) A substitutionary and representative sacrifice

Some scholars debate the details of what Paul means by the word 'redeemed'. Is there an understanding here simply of a price being paid, or of a sacrifice, or of Christ dying as our substitute while paying with his life for the death we deserved under God's judgment? Such discussions are interesting but ultimately miss the point here. Paul uses the words 'redemption', 'blood' and 'forgiveness' in close proximity. In this cascading prayer of praise to God, it is surely the case that these words are used as an appropriate shorthand for the whole means by which our election was secured **through Jesus Christ**. The **blood** reminds us that this was by sacrifice, even as the Exodus itself was achieved for all the 'sons of Israel' by means of a sacrificial lamb whose blood, when placed on the doorposts of a home, caused the avenging angel to 'pass by' without bringing death (Exod. 12:1-13). But it also reminds us that, in his death, Christ's sacrifice was sufficient and complete as a fulfilling of all that was required by God. All this was in order that we who were by nature objects of wrath and dead in transgressions (2:3, 5) might receive full **forgiveness** and be received as God's people, holy and blameless before him. Christ's death on the cross for all those throughout all the ages who would trust in him and become his people through God's grace, primarily involved Christ voluntarily taking the place of the sinner under God's judgment (substitution, see Eph. 5:2 and 5:25 and Gal. 3:13). Yet it is also described in representative terms, for again we may say that what is true of the King (who died and rose) is true of his people (who have died and been raised from the dead; see 2:5 and Gal. 2:20).

As Paul is caught up in praise, it is no wonder that he sees this as **the riches of God's grace**. In 1:18 he specifically prays that we will have our hearts enlightened to appreciate *the riches of his glorious inheritance.* (These 'riches' are also mentioned in 2:4, 7; 3:8, 16.) It is important to capture the 'feel' of Paul's excitement as he thinks through all that God's grace has achieved for us in Christ. Paul says that God **lavished** this upon us. The Greek word means something like 'he abundantly gave us', or 'he gave us more than we needed'. Surely here we are listening to Paul's joy! What redemption and forgiveness! What a life we really have 'in Christ'! We can virtually feel the tears arising within him as he sits in prison and thinks and speaks of the riches of God's grace.

iv) Part of God's great plan

God did all this **with all wisdom and understanding**[1] (v. 8). Once again Paul remembers that, wonder of wonders, this is all part of God's wise plan and purpose to bring glory to himself.

Sometimes studying the text in detail as we are here can seem very theoretical. We can study Paul's understanding of the saving work of Jesus, students can write an essay, others can speak on what they have learned to Bible study groups or some will preach on the passage. We can analyse the text, and all of this is valuable. Yet Paul wrote this theology with a thrill in his heart, and God's people must share this joy with Paul for it is a joy in God and his abundant grace. It is a joy focused not in ourselves but in him who chose us before the foundation of the world and predestined us in love to be part of his family.

---

1 Some commentators take this to refer to what God has given his people. But Paul's thinking here is centred on God and his plans.

e) The Mystery has been revealed in Christ (vv. 9-12)

In speaking of God's redemption in Christ and his forgiveness, Paul's thought again returns to the fact that this was God's plan all along. Until Christ came, it had remained a **mystery** how precisely God would fulfil his covenant promises to create a 'holy' people to himself and ensure their blamelessness. What also remained unexplained was how God would bless people from all over the earth, in fulfilment of his promises to Abraham. Thus, when Paul speaks of *mystery* he specially thinks about how, in Christ, God draws in the Gentiles to his people (see vv. 11-13 below, also 3:3-6, specially v. 6. Also Col. 1:27). This great will and purpose of God has been **put into effect**, it has been so ordered within God's plan, that it would all happen **when the times will have reached their fulfilment.**

This time of fulfilment has been ushered in by Christ the King. Now the gospel is going out to all the nations. Now people from all over the world are being saved in Christ. There is a great drawing together of the whole purpose of this world as Christ enters it and brings salvation. But this fulfilment is not yet complete, for Christ will return and bring this work to completion.

We might summarise the thought of verse 10 along these lines: The purposes of the world and its people seemed thwarted when Adam and Eve sinned. Disorder entered the ordered creation. The destiny of men and women was death rather than life. But it was always God's divine will to reveal his grace and love in Jesus Christ and to bring about a great restoration of order and of divine service. In Christ, this is what has happened, is happening, and will happen for the fulfilment of the ages is upon us. It involves **all things in heaven and on earth** because all that which is set against Christ has also been affected and will be dealt with in Christ as his exaltation as King makes clear (1:20-21).

Paul's joy is that **in him** (Christ) this mystery **has been made known**. It was always God's **will** and **good pleasure** that through Christ salvation would come not just to the Israelites or Jews but to the nations as well. It was always his will to exalt Christ and to deal with evil. The prophets had foretold this, but now it has been *revealed*. It is indeed God's plan to **'sum up' all things in Christ** (rather than NIV 'under one head, even Christ').

Paul now develops the idea of *all* Christians receiving the inheritance[2] that is God's will for them. Verse 11 refers to all Christians and Paul summarises the great truth that God has predestined them for a purpose **according to the plan. We, who were the first to hope in [the] Christ** refers at least to Paul and those early converts in Jerusalem and Judea, but probably to the gospel coming to the Jews first and then the Gentiles. In other words, Paul probably here identifies himself with the Jews who were the first to receive the gospel of the Messiah (Christ). They were called for **the praise of his glory** (see **b**) above). But **you also**, that is, those who had been converted in Ephesus and came from a largely Gentile background, have a part in all this.

Note that Paul equates **the word of truth** with **the gospel of your salvation.** As this truth was proclaimed and they **heard**, so they **believed** and received an equal standing with those who **were the first to hope in Christ.**

God is truly to be praised for the way the mystery was revealed. The Gentiles were drawn into the full privileges of being family members, *sons*, through hearing the gospel and believing in Christ.

f) Marked and sealed in Christ (vv. 13-14)

The Holy Spirit is the guarantee that all who are in Christ will receive their inheritance, and it is he who ensures that no distinctions are made between God's people. There are no first- and second-class people of God. We are all awaiting together that final day when Christ returns.

The work of redemption, the actual paying the cost and freeing from slavery to sin and transfer to another lordship, took place on the cross. That is where Satan was defeated,

---

2 Although the NIV says **in him we were also chosen**, the Greek word used here signifies being appointed to share in a lot. As we have noted when Paul uses the word *mystery* (v. 9), it is likely that he has in mind sharing in the inheritance that belongs to God's people. Thus ESV reads: 'In him we have obtained an inheritance, having been predestined...'

and here is the marvel of the Christian faith. It is firmly and essentially connected to historical reality, to real people, to a real God working in this world in its history, and to a real victory in the death and resurrection of Christ and his exaltation as Lord.

This redemption and salvation are experienced in the life of an individual when the word of truth is heard and people *believe*. At that point redemption is theirs and is sealed to them by the Holy Spirit. But what the Holy Spirit guarantees is that at the future day when Christ will return to judge, they will be *seen* to be redeemed. Paul even refers to the judgment day as *the day of redemption* in Ephesians 4:30. This is a wonderful thought. Christ's return, 'the day of the Lord', 'the day of wrath', the day of 'judgment', as the Bible variously describes it, can be spoken of by Christians as *the day of redemption*.

This work of the Spirit happens at conversion, **when you heard**... Some these days talk of a work of the Holy Spirit separate from the work of Christ. But on three accounts here that is shown to be incorrect. First, it is only 'in Christ' that we receive the Holy Spirit at all. Secondly, all who are 'in Christ' were sealed (past tense) with the Spirit, and thirdly, this is what was promised (**the Holy Spirit of promise**, v. 13). In other words, this is all part of the fulfilment of all covenant promises 'in Christ'. One of those promises was, as we know from Joel 2, that God would pour out his Spirit on all people. All Christians receive the Spirit as they come to Christ and find themselves 'in him'.

The idea of being **marked with a seal** is taken from the practice of slavery. Slaves were branded with a mark that was burned onto their flesh or even with a piece cut out of their ear. If a slave was sold he or she would have the mark of the new master put on them. Being sealed **in him** with the Holy Spirit again reminds us of a new Lordship. This is a sign of slavery to a new Lord. There are two lords to whom we can belong as human beings: either we belong to what Paul calls in 2:2 'the ruler of the kingdom of the air, the spirit who is now at work in those who are disobedient', or we belong to God the Father and to his Son Jesus Christ. When Christ the Lord takes possession of a person he has redeemed, he moves immediately to guarantee his slave's new status. He does this with his slave seal – the Holy Spirit. Now it is this Spirit who is at work in us, not any other.

But this slave-mark is also a sign of the Lord's protection. In Roman days slaves would be protected by their master. He was responsible for their welfare. In Scripture the work of the Spirit is undoubtedly about the welfare and protection of Christ's people. Thus the **guarantee** also means that God's people will be protected and kept for that final day to ensure they are still around to receive the inheritance that is theirs.

Paul returns at the end of this extraordinary outpouring of praise to what it is all about, to what the whole of history has been pointing, to what the election of a holy and blameless people was all for, and it is simply **to the praise of his glory**.

Further Application

First, we need to focus on Jesus and not on ourselves. How we need to recall the truth of these verses again and again, don't we? They are so practical and direct in their application to all our lives and yet they are full of the very deepest theology. We are chosen and loved and forgiven and redeemed so we can sing God's praise and give him all the glory. We are to be found 'in Christ', so we are inheritors with him of the divine promises and we are sealed by his Holy Spirit. Our whole culture these days pushes us towards focusing on ourselves. The truths to which this passage points take our gaze off ourselves and fix it where it should be: on God our Saviour. In this day and age we first and foremost must focus our hearts and minds on what it is to be 'in Christ'.

Secondly, freedom is not all it's cracked up to be! This passage speaks directly to the modern person seeking after 'freedom', freedom to do what we want, to be our own person, to act in whatever way makes us feel good. In fact, Christians often get really 'messed up' as they tend to define freedom, not in God's way, but in a way that has been defined by people living under another lordship, under the master of lies.

Sadly, of course, when people follow the 'other lord', they eventually discover the life they have lived has not been as rewarding as they had hoped. And they discover that they are not really 'free' for there are lots of people and circumstances that have power over them. Perhaps for some it is the callous employer, or perhaps difficult financial circumstances, or an addiction of some sort. Gradually they discover that the goals of this so-called 'free' world, goals of hedonism, self-promotion and so on are simply a dream.

The Biblical answer is to turn the whole question around. True freedom is found in one place only, by becoming a slave to Christ. At first glance, it seems that this cannot possibly be true because freedom and slavery are surely contradictory terms. But that is where the one true Lord, the Lord of all creation, speaks and says, 'Come to me, and I will give you rest.' In Matthew 11:19 we read: 'Take my yoke upon you and learn from me, for I am gentle and humble in heart, and you will find rest for your souls.'

There is an amazing little prayer in the Anglican prayer book and it has these words which beautifully summarise the Bible's teaching on freedom: 'In whose service is perfect freedom.' Paul shows us that true freedom is to be found in following the creator God himself, for then we fulfil our potential, then we know where we belong, there we know where to turn for help, there we know that we can even find the power to live. And it is all in the service of Christ, by becoming one of his sealed slaves, a converted person who is possessed by the Holy Spirit. The Lord protects his servants.

Finally, God's love addresses the alienation felt by so many in our society. 'Alienation' describes the feeling that so many have, that they do not belong anywhere, that they are not significant, that they have no purpose, that they are powerless to change their circumstances. Perhaps some of us have been like that. Perhaps, to some extent, you feel this as you read my words right now. It is at times like this, as we read passages like the one we have been studying, that we should let God speak to us.

This love of God does not depend on whether we are well thought of, nor on whether we have lots of friends, nor on whether we serve God as well as we might. God's love towards us, described here in this passage, is not determined by the sort of people we are or are not. 'He has blessed us with every spiritual blessing in Christ' as verse 3 puts it, because that is what he planned to do to demonstrate his love towards us. In Christ alone we find our true belonging as he draws us into covenant with him, as he places us in a family of his people, and as he gives us his Spirit to be with us and to protect us and guarantee our relationship with God himself in Jesus Christ.

Of course, it is one thing to know the theology and another to put it into practice in our own Christian lives. Yet if we call upon the Lord to help us overcome our feelings of alienation and powerlessness, so he, by the power of his Spirit within us, will work to change not just our life and behaviour but even our feelings. And we will come to know that, through his love, we *belong*.

A favourite modern hymn catches so clearly the joy of these opening verses of Ephesians.

> In Christ alone my hope is found,
> He is my strength, my light, my song;
> This corner stone, this solid ground,
> firm through the fiercest drought and storm.
> What heights of love, what depths of peace
> When fears are stilled, when strivings cease!
> My comforter, my All in All,
> Here in the love of Christ I stand.
>
> No guilt in life, no fear in death,
> This is the power of Christ in me;
> From life's first cry to final breath,
> Jesus commands my destiny.
> No power of hell, no scheme of man,
> Can ever pluck me from His hand;
> Till He returns or calls me home,
> Here in the power of Christ I'll stand![3]

---

3 Keith Getty & Stuart Townend, Copyright © 2001 Thankyou Music

3

Paul's first prayer for the Ephesian Christians
(Ephesians 1:15-23)

Paul finally breaks away from his great description of the blessings God's people have 'in Christ'. Now he becomes directly personal and tells them about his prayers for them and his thanksgiving to God for them.

a) A prayer of thanks for the Ephesian Christians (1:15-16)

> For this reason, ever since I heard about your faith in the Lord Jesus and your love for all the saints, I have not stopped giving thanks for you, remembering you in my prayers (1:15-16).

Paul's prayer is that these people will come to know God better as they ponder all that he has given them 'in Christ'. But he begins by telling them that he constantly gives thanks to the Lord for their **faith in the Lord Jesus** and their **love** for all God's people, **the saints**. Reports brought back to Paul have spoken of the deep faith of these people and their love and care for each other. It is a good indication of Paul's deep pastoral care for these Christians that he can talk of his regular prayers for them. There is nothing more needful for Christians than that they continue to seek a deeper and deeper understanding of God and his character and his working 'in Christ' on behalf of his people. Thanking God for a people exhibiting their Christian faith and praying for a deepening of their knowledge of God is a prayer that Christians should readily imitate as they pray for Christian friends.

b) A prayer that God will give them wisdom (vv. 17-19)
Paul prays that the Holy Spirit will enable God's people to know God the Father better.

> I keep asking that the God of our Lord Jesus Christ, the glorious Father, may give you the Spirit of wisdom and revelation, so that you may know him better (v. 17).

The glorious Father is literally *the Father of Glory* – a reminder that 'glory' is a description of the very character of God in all his awesome power, divinity, majesty and authority. By using this expression, Paul distinguishes between the Father and the Son, but he also shows what sort of **wisdom and revelation** is going to be needed if people are to know this God of Glory. It is only the Holy Spirit himself who will help God's people in this way. The depths and riches of all that God is and all that he has done is a treasure to be mined throughout this life until at last we see 'face to face'.

Christians have been given only a partial understanding of God, but it is one that will deepen as they mature in the faith. For Paul, the key need for everyone is to understand the wonder of what has been given in Christ. He wants everyone to get a grip on these great truths. He wants God's Spirit to give them wisdom and understanding that will help them praise God as they come to know him better in this way – as the one who has revealed all that it is necessary for us to know in this age. As Christians we still have to say with Paul in 1 Corinthians 13 that as yet we do not see it all, we see but dimly through a glass, but what we see, though never exhaustive of the great God of Glory, is utterly true for it has been revealed in Christ.

Paul now specifically prays that the Spirit-given wisdom and revelation will enlighten them in three areas.

> I pray also that the eyes of your heart may be enlightened in order that you may know the hope to which he has

called you, the riches of his glorious inheritance in the saints, and his incomparably great power for us who believe (1:18-19a).[1]

i) To know the hope to which they are called

Paul wants the Spirit to open their inner eyes, **the eyes of** their **heart**, so that people will really see the implications for the future of all that he has praised God for in the opening verses. God has chosen (v. 4), predestined, adopted (v. 5) and redeemed (v. 7) these people and so their future will be different. The **hope** to which Christians are called is the working out of God's plan 'to the praise of his glory' (v. 14). It will reach its great climax and fulfilment in the return of Christ in glory (see v. 10). It is partly enjoyed even at this present time through the deposit of the Holy Spirit and because all who are 'in Christ' continue to be protected and provided for even now.

The modern English use of the word 'hope' is very different from its use in Scripture. Nowadays when we talk of 'hope' we imagine that something may happen in the future, but then it might not! If it is my 'hope' that it will be sunny tomorrow, I know, when living in England, that this may be a forlorn hope! Now, living in Atlanta in June, July and August, I can 'hope' for a cool day, but that is certainly a forlorn hope! In Scripture, when this word is used in connection with the gospel and with the coming of Christ, it always carries certainty with it. The Christian's 'hope' in this sense is his or her 'expectation'. 'In Christ' our hope is certain, for he is the faithful one who fulfils his promises. In 4:4 we see that 'hope' summarises the gospel itself ('just as you were called to one hope when you were called'), and it becomes the basis on which Paul appeals for a worthy life to be lived in the present world (4:1).

ii) To know the riches of his inheritance in the saints

As children, many of us used to sing a very simple chorus. It went like this:

---

1 This verse continues on from the previous as one long sentence to the end of the chapter. The NIV makes it more readable by repeating 'I pray' and starting a new sentence.

Count your blessings,
Name them one by one,
And it will surprise you
what the Lord has done!

That is what Paul has been doing in this passage. He has been counting all the blessings he can think of in one long sentence. There are many he has not mentioned but he lists enough to provoke great joy and gratitude among all who read this epistle.

However, Paul now changes tack just a little. We have been thinking of *our* inheritance in Christ, but Paul now speaks of **his** (God's) **glorious inheritance in the saints**. God's people are seen as God's own inheritance. Paul is praying that Christians may understand that they, as God's people, the saints drawn from Jews and Gentiles alike, are hugely privileged. They are part of that which was always God's intention from before the foundation of the earth, namely, a people who would be 'holy and blameless' unto him. This is *his* inheritance and God himself finds it an inheritance 'of glory' (see on 3:21). How much more should we be amazed that God views us as his own inheritance.

As these Christians grow, Paul prays that they will come to see the privilege of their own place in God's plan. They are part of the glorious riches of what belongs to God. For us who are Christians in the twenty-first century this is our privilege as well, whatever earthly role God has called us to at this time, even if it is difficult and we do not much like it!

iii) To know his incomparable power
Why do we find it so hard to imagine that we can be *better* Christians? Perhaps it is often because we take our eyes off the ball. We think becoming better Christians or growing to be maturer Christians depends on us. We may have come to faith by grace, but now it is down to us!

What Paul says here is altogether different. All growth requires energy of some sort, but for this power Christian lives depend on the life-giving might of God that is at work within them. This is, of course, brought to us by God's Holy Spirit. The

Holy Spirit guarantees the inheritance, and brings us wisdom, revelation and enlightenment. Thus, the wonderful truth is that God himself takes us through this life, helping us grow and helping us through all the difficulties and temptations we face. He is determined to receive the glorious riches of *his* inheritance.

And so Paul reminds his readers that the real strength and power for changed and growing Christian lives (**for us who believe**) lies in God. There is nothing else like this **incomparably great power for us who believe**. And so Paul begins to describe this power in a way that ought to bring another thrill of excitement to all who read what he says.

c) The power of God in Christ (vv. 19b-23)

> That power is like the working of his mighty strength, which he exerted in Christ when he raised him from the dead and seated him at his right hand in the heavenly realms, far above all rule and authority, power and dominion, and every title that can be given, not only in the present age but also in the one to come. And God placed all things under his feet and appointed him to be head over everything for the church, which is his body, the fullness of him who fills everything in every way.

For emphasis here, Paul uses four different Greek words for this power of God **in Christ**. They all mean almost exactly the same thing. This power is so extraordinary that it is the same power that was used in the resurrection (**when he raised him from the dead**) and in the exaltation of Christ (**seated him at his right hand**).

As Paul thinks of this power he describes Christ's exaltation and is once again drawn into praise and thanksgiving.

i) Christ's position (vv. 20-21)
By God's great power, Jesus has been exalted to **the heavenly realms**, the place from which God rules, and has thus received glory and honour. See comments on 1:3 for a discussion of this phrase (used here, in 1:3 and in 2:6).

ii) Christ's authority

That he is **seated** at the Father's **right hand** reminds us of the authority that the Son has been given by the Father. This is **far above all rule and authority, power and dominion**. That is, the rule and authority of Christ are universal **not only in the present age but also in the one to come** (v. 21). At a practical level, it is important for all Christians to remember that Christ has universal authority even now. We do not have to await his return and the coming of the future age to experience and to know and enjoy his full authority as ascended Lord. Understanding the authority that belongs even now to Christ is important for a number of reasons. Principally it reminds us that he *is able to do immeasurably more than all we ask or imagine* (3:20). Because of Christ's authority it is possible to make *the most of every opportunity* even though *the days are evil* (5:16).

The Lord Jesus Christ is able to do what he wishes for his people, **for us who believe**. He is even able to deal with **all rule and authority**. These words are otherwise translated as *the rulers and authorities in the heavenly realms* in 3:10, but it is 6:20 that helps us understand what Paul has in mind here: 'For our struggle is not against flesh and blood, but against *the rulers, against the authorities,* against the powers of this dark world and against the spiritual forces of evil *in the heavenly realms*.'

Given the background of sorcery and magic at Ephesus (discussed in introduction), it seems more than likely that Paul has this in mind as he writes these verses. It was vital for these Christians to understand that Christ has all authority in spite of the power that they may perceive to be present in magic practices or in the worship of Artemis. Paul regards that power inherent in the world of darkness as real enough because Satan lies behind it all. However the encouragement is that Christ has all rule and authority, power and dominion ... in the present age.

Christ's authority is such that he has the victory both now (for his people), and in the future, over evil rulers and powers. We may struggle with them and the fight is serious, as we shall see when we come to chapter 6, but the Lord has already won the victory. His exaltation has given him authority over all, and this too must be a great encouragement to God's people that they are not alone, and that their fight is but a skirmish, for the victory is Christ's. The battle itself was won on the cross. This should provide us with extraordinary encouragement to live for him and follow him **in the present age**. But the future (**the age to come**) is his also. Christ's kingship will be seen in its full extent when he returns in glory.

And God placed all things under his feet and appointed him to be head over everything is a summary of what Paul has been saying. The words are drawn from Psalm 8:6 where we read: 'You made him ruler over the works of your hands; you put everything under his feet.' Christ is the complete fulfilment of the expectation of that psalm, and so many other Scriptures, that a king would come who would have universal authority. But the truly extraordinary fact that Christians need to know is that all of this is **for the church**. The *hope* of which Paul has talked in verse 18 can be fulfilled precisely because there is nothing anywhere that is not finally subject to Christ.

iii) Christ's headship over the church

Thus, Christ's authority is above all intended for the benefit and care of God's *inheritance in the saints*, the **church**. The death, resurrection and exaltation of Christ are part and parcel of God's (and Christ's) demonstration of extra-ordinary love for his people.[2] Paul is thinking here not just of the Ephesian Christians or the local churches of that area, but of the whole of God's church across the world and even his people of all ages (as he does whenever he uses the word in this letter). Christ has the position of **head**, of authority, **over the church**. We shall see as the letter progresses how important this theme of 'the church' will be to Paul's message.

Christ is so involved with his church that it is here described as **his body**. This picture is used elsewhere by the apostle, and it draws attention to the close relationship of Christ to his people. He is united with them and they with him and with

---

2 This emphasis on God's love for the people called and destined to be his church recurs many times in this letter. For example, 1:5; 2:4; 3:19; 5:1-2 etc.

each other.[3] But Christ remains distinct and the **head** over the church as much as over **everything** else.

The last part of verse 23 is truly difficult! **... the fullness of him who fills everything in every way.** Many have debated its meaning. Put briefly we may ask whether it is the church that is the fullness of God, or Christ who is the fullness of God? Without going into detail about these discussions, it seems more likely (at least to this writer) that **fullness** describes the church.[4] One reason for thinking this is that Paul prays that the church may receive this fullness in 3:19 – '*that you may be filled to the measure of all the fullness of God*'.

In other words, the church is **Christ's body** and also is **the fullness of Christ**... But we need to ask just what this means. Even though Christ **fills everything in every way,** even though he has all authority and power and gives his church *grace upon grace from his fullness* (John 1:16), even though we have yet to attain the *fullness of Christ* (Eph. 4:13), Christ finds himself 'complete' as his Church is perfected. Ephesians 5:25-32 perhaps gives us some help in seeing this. Just as a husband needs his wife for the two to become one flesh, so Christ and his church are to be united. Precisely because God's people, the church, were called before the foundation of the world *in Christ*, and precisely because Christ has all authority *for the church*, Christ *without* the church has something missing.[5]

Calvin carefully summarises this: 'This is the highest honour of the Church, that, unless He is united to us, the Son of God reckons Himself in some measure imperfect.'[6] To put it another way, and picking up on the picture of Ephesians 5, the bride provides the *fullness* for the groom. Even so, lest we might think that Christ somehow *needs* us to be fully the Son

---

3 This does not at all imply that the church is somehow an extension of the literal Christ, as is suggested in some Christian traditions.

4 For a very detailed discussion which ends up taking a different view, see A Lincoln (1990), *Ephesians*, Word Biblical Commentary, Word Books, pp. 71-78.

5 Of course, Christ is still Christ and still divine, and still the Son without the church. That is why Paul adds that he is the one *who fills everything in every way*. Nevertheless, the goal of his work and his power and authority is that the church will be *his* body, united with him.

6 J. Calvin, *Ephesians*, p. 138.

of God, Paul reminds us as he finishes that Christ remains **the fullness of him** [God] **who fills everything in every way**.

Summary of Chapter 1

Paul has begun this letter with a description of the extraordinary plan of God for his people and the blessings that they have been given 'in Christ'. The passage shows the depth of God's grace and love for his people who are his 'inheritance'. Chosen and loved in accordance with God's great and wise plan, Christians have been marked and sealed with the gift of the promised Holy Spirit.

The last verses of the chapter have not been easy, but Paul's prayer for these Christians has first and foremost been that they will all come to know God better. He prays that the Holy Spirit will continually enlighten them so that they will know the hope to which they are called and come to appreciate ever more deeply the extraordinary place that they have as God's people, for they are *his* inheritance. Paul also prays that they may know and experience the great power of God in Christ and, as he reflects on this, Paul begins to describe Christ's power, glory, authority and, above all, his headship over the church. Yet, though head over the church, his relationship with the church is intimate and very deep indeed. The church is thus described as Christ's *body*. Paul wants these Christians to know that Christ's power over all things is *for* them. They will triumph because he has triumphed, and so there is no need to be disheartened as they face a world of magic, false gods, of opposition and even persecution.

4

Made alive by God's grace
(Ephesians 2:1-10)

Paul has spoken at length of the Christian's great inheritance 'in Christ'. He has talked of Christ's power used for the sake of his people, and has poured out his thanksgiving and praise to God for all that he has done for the church. He has prayed that these Christians will grow in their knowledge and experience as well as in appreciation of all that God has done, is doing and will do on their behalf in Christ. But now Paul reminds them of their context and background. No Christians should ever become arrogant or proud because God has done all this for them. It is because of God's great and wonderful mercy and grace, and because of this alone, that people find themselves 'in Christ' and part of his church.

This remarkable love, mercy and power of Christ has already been experienced by these Christians, specially when they consider what they *were*.

a) By Nature: Dead in your sins (2:1-3)

As for you, you were dead in your transgressions and sins, in which you used to live when you followed the ways of this world and of the ruler of the kingdom of the air, the spirit who is now at work in those who are disobedient. All of us also lived among them at one time, gratifying the cravings of our sinful nature and following its desires and thoughts. Like the rest, we were by nature objects of wrath (2:1-3).

Paul simply begins (Greek) 'And you were dead...' The link with what has gone before is established. They were **dead in transgressions and sins**.[1] Paul's statement about the spiritual condition of men and women is stark. He does not say that they *were dying*, nor does he suggest that they were at their wit's end. He does not say that they were longing for spiritual enlightenment. There is no indication here that these people could have made themselves alive. Rather, they were **dead** spiritually. And the simple fact is that dead people do not come alive again, at least not without God's miraculous intervention.

The fact that they were dead spiritually is established by how they **used to live** physically. The word Paul actually employs here is 'used to *walk*'. The verb *to walk* is regularly used in the New Testament to indicate the way people live their lives and what they do in this world with their lives. This becomes important later in the letter, in chapters 4 and 5, as we learn how Christians themselves are to *walk* in direct contrast with how the spiritually dead *walk*.[2] While some *walk* in sin, this section will end with a joyful reminder to Christians that God has specially prepared good works for them *to walk in* (2:10). The type of life or walking that is symptomatic of those who are spiritually dead is found firstly in whom they follow, and secondly in their life priorities. Their end is judgment by God.

i) Following the ruler of the kingdom of the air

When we discussed the nature of redemption back in 1:7 we considered the transfer of lordships that takes place as a person becomes a Christian and is 'redeemed'. Here Paul describes the **ruler** under whom those who are not Christ's live. He is the **ruler of the kingdom of the air**.... In 1:21 we have already seen that there are supernatural powers opposed to the Lord, and this is a description of such powers, but personalised to refer to the one who leads all such powers, Satan himself. In 4:27 and in 6:11 Paul calls him the Devil. He has a limited

---

1 There is no substantial difference between these two words.
2 For example, 4:1, 17; 5:2, 8, 15 etc.

kingdom ('authority' in Greek). It is described as **of the air** which is a description of those spiritual realms where Satan holds sway. It is the same as what Paul calls in Colossians 1:13 *the dominion* ('authority' in Greek) *of darkness.*

The fact that people either follow one lord or another is further emphasised in the description that follows – **the spirit who is now at work in those who are disobedient**. Again the personal agency of Satan behind all that is evil is in mind, and it is this **spirit** that is at work in those who are spiritually dead, **who are disobedient.**[3]

We can now see clearly what is meant in verse 2 when we read, **when you followed the ways of this world.** It is a description of following the ways of the kingdom of evil. In fact the word used is *'the age* of this world', reminding us of the contrast between *the present age* and the *age to come* that was spoken of in 1:21.

ii) Following a sinful nature
The symptoms that all Christians can identify as indicating death are those that were once found among **all of us.** Paul knows he too gratified the **cravings** of the **sinful nature** (Greek: 'flesh') and followed **its desires and thoughts.** Elsewhere Paul contrasts life in the Spirit with following the 'flesh', and that is what he has in mind here. Paul knows that this nature is one that is spiritually dead, for it leads to thoughts and actions that are opposed to God and obeying him. This is why Paul has just called such people **disobedient.** Those who follow Satan find that their whole life is preoccupied with self-gratification, not only in what they do but also in the way they think. This is the way of **this world**, which is one that is wholly set against God. People do not even realise that they are **dead!** Their priority is themselves, although what in fact they fail to realise is that all of this is driven on by the **ruler of the kingdom of the air**. It is not much wonder that people find themselves under God's judgment.

---

3 Greek: '*sons of disobedience*'. As with adopted sons of God, sonship implies family resemblance.

iii) Objects of wrath

Many, perhaps the majority, of those addressed in this letter were converted Gentiles (v. 11), but here Paul makes clear that, whether their background had been Jew or Gentile, they were in the same boat, as he says in verse 3, **Like the rest, we**... The apostle is stating clearly that without Christ all people are spiritually dead and without hope. It is not as if Paul, because of his background as a leading Jew and theologian, was somehow at least partly 'alive'. As we shall see in verse 5, he too needed to be *made alive*. Paul's argument is reminiscent of the opening chapters in Romans where the desperate plight of Gentiles is discussed as they are seen to refuse any notion of the true God, but where Paul then goes on to point out that Jews are in the same predicament:

> What shall we conclude then? Are we any better? Not at all! We have already made the charge that Jews and Gentiles alike are all under sin. As it is written: 'There is no one righteous, not even one; there is no one who understands, no one who seeks God' (Rom. 3:9-11).

In fact, all of us **were by nature objects of wrath**. Paul uses the word *children of wrath* here. Clearly they are the same people who are described as *the sons of disobedience* in verse 2. In other words, every one of us stood under the judgment (**wrath**) of God.

God's 'wrath' or 'anger' with sinners is not in any sense the type of anger that we might have that is so often arbitrary and, of course, quite sinful. We are often 'blinded' by anger. We cannot see what is true and what is untrue, we become irrational. Our anger is often self-centred. God's wrath is altogether different. The word describes his judicial righteousness that expresses his full opposition to those who sin and to their way of life. As the Judge of all and as one who is perfectly righteous and holy and sees things as they really are, God's justice demands his judgment of condemnation on those who sin.

All are **by nature** under such judgment. The same phrase is used in Galatians 2:15 where we read: 'We who are Jews *by nature*...' The NIV translates that verse as 'by birth', and this is clearly what Paul has in mind in Ephesians as well. Although Paul does not pause here to explain how it all comes about that human beings are born with and into sin, he does so in Romans 5:12-21. There he explains that human beings, as descendants of the first sinner Adam, are under the same judgment. We are all born as a people who are **by nature objects** (children) **of wrath**. This helps explain why Paul sees all who are without Christ as *dead*. As he says in Romans 5:12: 'just as sin entered the world through one man, and death through sin, and in this way death came to all men, because all sinned...' In other words, we are all outside 'the garden of Eden', all following the ways of Adam and Eve, all under God's judgment.

So by using the two words **by nature**, Paul is asserting that it is part and parcel of being born a human being to find ourselves under God's judgment. This then is the setting into which the great love, mercy and forgiveness of God breaks through 'in Christ'. It is only when we understand truly who and what we *were*, that we will come to understand the depths of God's love and grace that Paul now goes on to expound.

b) By grace: made alive with Christ (vv. 4-10)

The next few verses are surely among the most wonderful in all of Scripture. Here, in a few short words, Paul expresses the heart of the glory of the gospel. Here he speaks of salvation with all its joy and expounds on that most wonderful of words in Christian vocabulary: **grace**. Paul shows us that the only hope for those who are spiritually dead is a miracle that comes from outside them. The spiritually dead have no power within themselves to change their circumstances, but rather God raises them together by the resurrection of his Son, Jesus Christ.

> But because of his great love for us, God, who is rich in mercy, made us alive with Christ even when we were dead in transgressions ... (vv. 4-5a).

i) God's love and mercy

God alone is the answer to the problem that humanity faces. And Paul begins: **But God who is rich in mercy**. It is here that he and the Christians around Ephesus, and indeed around the world, have found the only available answer. We have a merciful God who has **loved** us. The Greek gives us a double emphasis on this: 'through the great *love* with which he *loved* us.' We mentioned earlier how this epistle repeatedly affirms God's love for his people, and no passage in the whole of Scripture does it more clearly than this one. But more than just love is required if people are to be made alive. The word **mercy** is also critical.

Never in Scripture is God portrayed as one who compromises one side of his character for the sake of another. His justice is not compromised for the sake of his extraordinary love. It is part of God's character that he is also prepared to be merciful. His mercy is of course shown 'in Christ'. As Christ voluntarily dies on the cross for his people, he does so under the 'wrath' or judgment of God. Paul does not expound this here, simply saying that he **made us alive** *with* **Christ,** but we saw a little of what was involved when he spoke of redemption through Christ's blood in 1:7.

God's love and mercy are the grounds of all that subsequently happens to achieve salvation for those who are dead in sin. At the top of Paul's mind here, however, is the glorious fact that the impossible has happened, people have been **made alive, even when** they **were dead in transgressions,** and it is all down to the amazing love and mercy of God himself.

ii) God's grace

– it is by grace you have been saved... For it is by grace you have been saved (2:5b-8a).

The word which best summarises all of God's love and mercy to the spiritually dead is the word *grace*. This word appears six times in these two opening chapters and eleven times in the whole epistle. We have already defined it when looking at the opening two verses of the book. Here Paul is emphatic and repeats the truth so necessary for all Christians to understand.

Grace adds a very special element to the words 'love' and 'mercy'. It is this word that specially incorporates the understanding that the recipients did not deserve what they were being given. It is the word which thus adds emphasis to the notion of being 'dead' before being 'made alive'. Being saved therefore is all of God and is not of us. Unless we grasp this fact of grace, as well as the depths of God's love and mercy, we shall run the risk of thinking that perhaps, just perhaps, we might have done something of ourselves to gain or even to earn our salvation. Paul's rejoicing and thanksgiving to God in the first chapter, and his joy as he recounts the gospel of salvation in this chapter, is precisely because it is all of God.

iii) God's salvation

– it is by grace you have been saved. And God raised us up with Christ and seated us with him in the heavenly realms in Christ Jesus (2:5b-6).

Saved is a word which describes well the rescuing from death to life. It is a shorthand for all of which Paul has been talking. But it specially has to do with being saved from the wrath or judgment of God. First, we should note that Paul does not say that 'we have saved ourselves'. Rather the passive (**have been**) is used. This was done to Christians by God. God's grace did not make it possible for us now to save ourselves. Rather, God in his grace achieved the salvation on our behalf in Christ.

Salvation in the New Testament can sometimes be spoken of in the past tense, or in the present tense, and most often in the future tense. When it is in the future tense, then it usually looks forward to the second coming of Christ to judge when we shall find that all those who believe will be saved. In other words they will be spared judgment, God's wrath, and find redemption.[4] When it is in the present tense it normally describes the current experience of Christians who are to live godly lives because they live knowing that their salvation is

---

4 For example, Romans 5:9: 'Since we have now been justified by his blood, how much more shall we be saved from God's wrath through him!'

secure and guaranteed.[5] Here in Ephesians 2 Paul speaks of having been saved in the past. He is thinking of the continuing impact in the Christian's life of all that was achieved **in Christ Jesus** on their behalf when he died on the cross and was raised by God.

When Paul talks of what we have 'in Christ' he regularly uses verbs in Greek which have a prefix meaning 'together with' and we find three of them here in verses 5 and 6: God 'made us alive together with' Christ, God 'raised us together with' Christ, and God 'seated us together with' Christ in the heavenly realms in Christ Jesus.

We pointed towards a quite remarkable fact earlier when we looked at 1:1. Being 'in Christ' sums up all that Christians have and are as 'co-heirs' with Christ (Rom. 8:17), as his people. These 'together with' words help us to see that our inheritance in Christ is so deep and wonderful that we can summarise it like this: *What is true of our King Jesus is true of us.* They point to the fact that Christ is truly our representative King. He brings us before God. He is alive, he has been raised, therefore his people are alive and have been raised together with him. He is seated in the **heavenly realms**, therefore we are **seated together with him**.

It is one thing to understand that we are **made alive**, or even that we are **raised up with Christ**, but believing that we **are seated with him in the heavenly realms** requires a degree more effort. Most Christians do not feel this is true of them day by day. We all continue to struggle with this world, we find life hard and being a Christian very hard. We do not easily imagine that we are with Christ in the heavenly realms! Colossians 3:1-3 can help us understand this:

> Since, then, you have been raised with Christ, set your hearts on things above, where Christ is seated at the right hand of God. Set your minds on things above, not on earthly things. For you died, and your life is now hidden with Christ in God.

---

5 For example, 1 Corinthians 1:18; see also Philippians 2:12.

The basic idea is back to the question of 'lordships' which we have discussed earlier. In becoming a Christian and being saved, people have been moved from the kingdom of darkness to the kingdom of Christ. They share already in Christ's victory over the powers of Satan. They enjoy the knowledge that Jesus is enthroned and all powerful, even as they continue to live in the often hard circumstances of this world. A Christian's focus, even now, should be on the victory already obtained for them and they should rejoice that being 'in Christ', and represented by him in the glory of his enthronement, means they already inhabit a different spiritual reality from the one in which they were spiritually dead. Now we find ourselves raised and seated with Christ.

Ephesians 3:10-11 can further help us here:

> His intent was that now, through the church, the manifold wisdom of God should be made known to the rulers and authorities in the heavenly realms, according to his eternal purpose which he accomplished in Christ Jesus our Lord.

Although the **coming age**, the age ushered in by the return of Christ, will see the full manifestation of the riches of God's grace, yet even now the church is a witness to it. In that sense it prefigures now on this earth what is to come.

iv) God's gift

> ...in order that in the coming ages he might show the incomparable riches of his grace, expressed in his kindness to us in Christ Jesus. For it is by grace you have been saved, through faith – and this not from yourselves, it is the gift of God – not by works, so that no one can boast (2:7-9).

Already we have seen how God calls into being a people who will belong to him and be holy and blameless. We have seen that this is all done to his own great praise and glory (see comments on 1:4 above). The end of verse 7 now summarises this. He has saved a people **in Christ Jesus in order that** the **incomparable riches of his grace** will be shown to them all throughout eternity. The **kindness** of God remains permanently on view in and through the redeemed and it will always redound to his glory.

And so as Paul draws to a close this great expression of gratitude and praise at the grace of God in Christ, he repeats his emphasis on grace and explains it a little further. The means by which grace is received is **through faith** (also see 3:12, 17). It is clear that we cannot see 'faith' as the bit that we do in order to be saved! That is why Paul stresses the **gift** nature of salvation and that it is **not by works**, and so **no one can boast**. No one can claim that they somehow did something that deserved the grace they have been given. Both grace and faith are gifts of God.

There is some discussion here about the phrase **and this not from yourselves**. To what does **this** refer? Is it faith or the general fact of salvation that Paul has in mind? Though it does not make a lot of difference to Paul's intention, it is likely that it is to the whole fact of the grace-nature of salvation that Paul is referring. In other words, we might put it like this: 'It is by grace you have been saved, through faith, and (this) your whole salvation is not from yourselves, but is a gift from God, not from works...' Paul's meaning is that everything that he has been describing that has to do with our salvation has to do with God and his initiative, and does not come from ourselves. This includes faith itself.[6]

If the unregenerate person is constantly, in effect, putting himself or herself in the place of God, the regenerate, believing Christian needs to realise just how prone he or she is to this temptation. Time and again we want to put ourselves in the place of God; time and again we are tempted to pride. We may not always speak of it in this way. But the reality in the lives of most Christians is that we constantly want to think that *somehow* we have deserved salvation. We are tempted to be proud, to **boast** of what we now are and what we have achieved. We are always thinking of what *we* do for the Lord or for others around us. *We* believed, *we* went forward at that evangelistic meeting, *we* gave our lives to Christ and so on. In

---

6 Elsewhere this point that faith itself is part of the gift is made explicit, for example, in Acts 13:48; 14:27; 18:27.

some senses all these statements are true, and yet the way we emphasise our part in this saving work of God often removes us far from where the apostle Paul wants us to be as he writes this section of Ephesians.

Our salvation has not been achieved **by works**, that is, by anything we do or contribute. We cannot boast. Rather Paul wants us to look with praise and thanksgiving to the God who has brought us the most incomparable riches in Christ, which riches include the whole of our salvation, and even the *means* by which that salvation is applied to us, the means of faith. This is not just some abstract theologising about the place of faith in salvation, rather it is about putting God first in *all* our thinking about our salvation. Only when we do this will we understand why Paul is so excited about the nature of God's saving **grace**. Though undeserving, spiritually dead sinners, 'in Christ' God took the initiative to bring us to life, to raise us up, and to seat us with Christ in the heavenlies. How **incomparable** are the **riches of his grace**! How deep is the **great love with which he loved us**! How **rich in mercy** he is! What **kindness** has he **expressed to us in Christ Jesus**!

If our works have had no part in our salvation, we must ask what place there is in God's purposes for what we *do*. And remarkably we now find that there is a place for works, but even this is of grace.

v) God's workmanship

> For we are God's workmanship, created in Christ Jesus to do good works, which God prepared in advance for us to do (2:10).

Psalm 116:12 asks: *How can I repay the LORD for all his goodness to me?* If it is all of grace, then we are indeed left asking this question. How are God's people expected to respond to such love, mercy and grace? So often it seems that we can take it all for granted. Yet surely it is worth noting that, in the one and a half chapters in which Paul has been looking at the riches of the heavenly blessings we have in Christ, he has said hardly a word about how Christians are to behave or about them doing anything for the Lord.

However, at last he comes briefly to this question, which he will return to later, and refers to **good works**. The people chosen, called, and redeemed, as he has described them, are for God's praise and glory. They have been raised from spiritual death to life in Christ. They are thus very literally **God's workmanship** *created* **in Christ Jesus**. This is the climax towards which Paul has been leading. We are new creations in Christ.

In the New Testament we are familiar with a number of expressions that describe this radical newness of the one who has moved from the kingdom of darkness to the kingdom of light. In John 3:3, 7 Jesus referred to it as being 'born again'. Peter uses the same expression in 1 Peter 1:23. Paul's favoured description centres on the idea of creation. In 2 Corinthians 5:17-18 he again links grace with ideas of creation: 'Therefore, if anyone is in Christ, he is a new creation; the old has gone, the new has come! All this is from God...' Likewise, in Galatians 6:15 we read, 'Neither circumcision nor uncircumcision means anything; what counts is a new creation'. Later, when Paul does indeed move on in Ephesians to talk of how Christians should live and behave, he reminds them in 4:24 that new creatures have a new nature and should live accordingly: 'put on the new self, created to be like God in true righteousness and holiness.'

We must not underestimate the significance of this idea of 'creation'. Paul has already talked of the *power* (1:19) that God has applied to our lives, the same power that raised Christ back to life from the dead. This power that takes what is dead and makes it alive is rightly seen as God's *creative* power. And there has been a purpose behind all this creative activity. God has brought his people into being and fashioned them in such a way that, though not saved by works, they will now do works (the same word in v. 10 as in v. 9). And because they are *created in Christ Jesus* these will of necessity be **good works**. That is, they will be works produced by a people whom God has brought into being to do *his* will, to follow *his* good purposes.

Even more remarkable is that these very works, by which Christians may indeed respond to the grace of God, are themselves part of God's gracious provision for his people, for he has *prepared* **them in advance**. As we read this we may recall 1:3 where Paul talked of Christians being chosen in Christ *before the creation of the world to be holy and blameless in his sight*. Even in that verse there is an assumption that God always had a purpose wholly planned out for the existence of this people that he would bring into being. The good works that Paul now refers to are surely all that God has always planned should be done by a people who are holy and blameless. We can offer no excuse as God's new creation for failing to be the people God has called us to be, for he has graciously planned out even what we should be doing with our lives to be the people he wants us to be. God does have a will for the day-to-day lives of his people and, as we shall see later in the letter, our job is to follow that will and reflect the fact that we are new creations following a divine plan of work that will bring still further glory to the Creator.

5

A holy temple in the Lord
(Ephesians 2:11-22)

The next twelve verses continue to discuss the extraordinary change that has come to pass in the lives of those who are saved by grace. In verses 1-10 the contrast was drawn between being dead in sin and being by nature children of wrath with being in Christ and receiving the incomparable riches of God's grace. In the verses that follow the contrast between then and now is still just as evident, but Paul instead stresses the privilege of moving from being outside the community of God's people to finding Jew and Gentile united within that community: the church. One of the obvious links with what has gone before is that this new situation is again linked to God's creative power (v. 15).

a) Gentiles were separated from God (2:11-12)

> Therefore, remember that formerly you who are Gentiles by birth and called 'uncircumcised' by those who call themselves 'the circumcision' (that done in the body by the hands of men) – remember that at that time you were separate from Christ, excluded from citizenship in Israel and foreigners to the covenants of the promise, without hope and without God in the world (2:11-12).

Paul now addresses those who have converted from paganism, those who were not Jews but Gentiles. In a rather derogatory way, Jews had called such people 'the uncircumcised'. For

Jews the badge or marker of membership among God's people was their circumcision which had indicated, first, obedience to God's command to Abraham and, secondly, membership of and commitment to the God of the covenant.

The change that Christian Gentiles have seen is truly remarkable and they should **remember** what they were formerly. This idea of *remembering* is one that should characterise Christians of all ages. There is of course first and foremost the 'remembering' that we engage in as we take communion and remember how and at what cost our redemption and forgiveness was won by Christ. But we should also remember *from* what we were saved, for this drives us to thanksgiving and praise and to a deeper recognition of God's grace in taking us from **without hope** to being **near** to God.

Paul builds up the sense of distance from God by listing three ways in which Gentiles were **far away**. First, they were **separate from Christ**. It was one of the privileges of the people of Israel, and one of the great covenant promises that the Messiah would come from their race. Gentiles did not even have this to look forward to.

Secondly, they were **excluded from citizenship in Israel and foreigners to the covenants of the promise**. The apostle is quite clear that there were real advantages to being a Jew. There was a closeness to God brought about through the covenants that he had made with the people of Israel. Their privileges in a covenantal relationship with God were great. God had shown his presence to them in the tabernacle and in the temple. He had given them his law by which they should live. He had spoken to them through his prophets. But he had also made amazing promises to them (**covenants of the promise**). He had promised that his people would bring blessings to the whole world, that a King would sit on David's throne for ever, that the Holy Spirit would be poured out on them, that the Messiah would come. Citizenship of Israel, established through circumcision and commitment to the covenant Lord himself, brought with it a genuine closeness to and relationship with God which Gentiles did not enjoy.

Then, thirdly, they were **without hope and without God in the world**. They lived *in the world*. This means that they lived lives that did not follow God, reminding us of 2:2. He was not part of their thinking or their life. They were without hope, because God alone, as we have seen through the whole epistle thus far, can bring hope and salvation by his grace.

b) Gentiles are near to God in Christ (2:13)

> But now in Christ Jesus you who once were far away have been brought near through the blood of Christ.

After such an indictment of their previous condition, the contrast with their current position before God is all the more astonishing. As in 2:4 where Paul suddenly shows the contrast between then and now by saying 'but ... God', so here he does it again. He changes tack and says **'but...'** The difference in the lives of these Gentiles is that they have **now** been caught up **in Christ Jesus**. Those who **were far away** from God **have been brought near**.

This verse also reminds Gentiles how it is that they have been brought near to God: **through the blood of Christ**. It was through the sacrificial death of Christ on the cross that their salvation has been procured, reminding us of what Paul had already said in 1:7 (see comments on that verse).

For those of us who have grown up mostly knowing Christians who have come from a non-Jewish background, it is specially important that we grasp the impact of what the apostle says here. We take it for granted that 'anyone' can become a Christian. We forget just how amazing is God's electing grace, and we need to *remember* what things were like or would have been like without God and without now being 'in Christ'. Pausing to think about this from time to time will cause us to give more thanks to the Lord for his mercy and love, but also to think about all those who have not so far heard of the Lord's salvation and who also need to be 'brought near'.

The fact is that the marvellous creative power of God has been at work to bring us (who were not only dead but also without hope, far away, and excluded from the one nation where the true God had revealed himself and had made promises of salvation) close to God, and to bring us into his covenant community, the church. It is this idea that Paul will soon develop.

c) Peace in Christ (2:14-18)

> For he himself is our peace, who has made the two one and has destroyed the barrier, the dividing wall of hostility, by abolishing in his flesh the law with its commandments and regulations (2:14-15a).

Emphatically Paul says, *Christ* (**he himself**) is our peace. If Jew and Gentile had been separated as peoples, the one with a covenantal relationship with God and the other 'far away', Christ has now **destroyed** that **barrier** of 'farness' and 'closeness'. In Christ, Jew and Gentile have been brought together into **one** people.

i) *The dividing wall of hostility*

The **dividing wall** between Jew and Gentile was seen in a number of obvious ways. The **law** provided one such great barrier. In fact Paul goes on to speak of **the law with its commandments and regulations**. Part of the purpose of the law was deliberately to show what a 'holy' people were like, and they were a people separated away from the rest of the world, living in a certain God-appointed way and enjoying his covenant promises and protection. The law clearly divided those within the *covenants of promise* from those without. Not only that, but the law was also the evidence in itself that the people of Israel had come near to God (through their representative Moses) and that he had spoken to them in a way that he had not spoken to other nations. Circumcision was another dividing mark to which Paul has already referred in verse 11.

The exclusion of Gentiles from being able to 'come near' was also clearly demonstrated in the temple itself, and it is this that is most likely to be what Paul has in mind.[1] At the heart

---

1 This is made the more likely since in verse 18 Paul notes that this peace brings 'access' to the Father. We believe that Ephesians was written by Paul and therefore not to be dated later than the early sixties. There is therefore no reason why, as some suggest, the temple itself could not have been in Paul's mind as he wrote.

of the temple was the place where, symbolically, God had his presence on this earth in a special way, in the Holy of Holies. Even God-fearing Gentiles could only come into the outer courts of the temple. Even they could not come as near to God as their Jewish friends could. In reality there was a dividing wall of hostility right in the temple. This separated the Court of the Gentiles from the courts that were closer to the most holy place. In the late nineteenth century a temple pillar was found with an inscription which warned people that 'no one of another race is to enter within the fence'. Surely nothing could have been a more vivid reminder of the separation and hostility between Jew and Gentile. Nothing could have been a stronger reminder that one group was highly privileged and the other not.

ii) Jew and Gentile reconciled in Christ

With this background in mind, Gentiles should be even more aware of the joys of what has happened **now in Christ Jesus**. He **has destroyed the barrier**, the **wall**. And this has produced two amazing results. The first is, as we have seen, that Gentiles have been *brought near*. But the second is also of vital concern to us all: Christ has created **one new man out of the two**. There is reconciliation between Jew and Gentile so that such distinctions on the basis of race or history no longer count for anything.

His purpose was to create in himself one new man out of the two, thus making peace (2:15b). For those, Jew and Gentile, who are 'in Christ' there is a new peace that gets rid of the divisions and hostilities. Notice again how this is regarded as a 'creating' act by God. Such a peace-making could only happen at the hand of God in Christ. Something new has been formed, and it was **his purpose** to make **one new man**. The 'newness' of what is created is important, for the assumption remains from the first part of the chapter that, 'in Christ', all this has happened to spiritually 'dead' people, whether Jew or Gentile. What is created is a new living society or organism or **body** (v. 16) which is at peace with itself. No longer is one 'near' and the other 'far away', and no longer need one be called the 'circumcision' and the other the 'uncircumcision', for, as God had purposed, they have been brought together in peace.

Furthermore, and most importantly, this **one** new body is also at peace with God.

iii) Jew and Gentile reconciled to God

> ... in this one body to reconcile both of them to God through the cross, by which he put to death their hostility. He came and preached peace to you who were far away and peace to those who were near. For through him we both have access to the Father by one Spirit (2:16-18).

This is the second achievement of Christ being *our peace and breaking down the wall of hostility*. The first was that he might reconcile Jew and Gentile. The second is that he might **reconcile both of them to God**. Thus, **both of them**, Jew and Gentile, have peace with God. Where once both groups had been under God's wrath (2:3), now both are **reconciled to God.** 'Reconciliation' is a word that speaks to the bringing together of warring parties. Scriptures are clear that all men and women are in a relationship with God. Those who believe in Christ are at peace with God and experience his grace at first hand, while those who do not are 'enemies' of God. In Romans 5:10 Paul spells this out as he speaks of the Christian's previous state and of the true nature of salvation: 'For if, when we were God's enemies, we were reconciled to him through the death of his Son, how much more, having been reconciled, shall we be saved through his life!'

This 'peace treaty' with God is crucial to the whole matter of our salvation. It comes back to the issue of 'lordships' of which we have talked earlier. The Bible portrays Satan as the 'other lord' who wars against God and his people. Those who follow him are, therefore, also at war with God even if they are unknowingly being used by Satan in this way. Salvation must therefore be salvation from the final defeat of Satan and his forces by Christ. Put in a nut-shell, salvation means being saved *from* God as Christ returns in full victory to destroy the enemy, mete out God's justice and vindicate his people.

Reconciliation with God, peace with God, is therefore one of the vital components of what we have 'in Christ'.

Once again Paul reminds us that this was achieved **through the cross.** In other words, Christ's sacrificial death in our place took the wrath that we deserved. But we must not forget in all this that, even while we are still enemies, God is the one who is bringing about the reconciliation. It is by his initiative and by the work of Christ that our peace is achieved. Hence Paul says, **he himself is our peace.**

Paul further explains what has happened by saying that Christ **came and preached peace to you who were far away and peace to those who were near.** Paul sees in the work of Christ a fulfilment of prophecy, specially the prophecies of Isaiah. Thus, in his summary, he draws together Isaiah 52:7 ('How beautiful on the mountains are the feet of those who bring good news, who proclaim peace, who bring good tidings, who proclaim salvation, who say to Zion, "Your God reigns!"') with Isaiah 57:19 ('Peace, peace, to those far and near," says the LORD. "And I will heal them"'). Christ is the 'good news' that is preached, and he brings peace to both those who are far and those who are near.

The end result, indeed the whole goal of the peace that the new **one body** has received **through** Christ, is that **we both have access to the Father.** In a clear Trinitarian statement, Paul tells us this access happens by means of **one Spirit.** The Holy Spirit who takes up residence in God's people enables and empowers their approach to the Father in worship. As we are later told in 4:4: 'There is one body and one Spirit' (see also 1 Cor. 12:13).

d) Members of God's household (2:19-22)

The result of this new unity in the one body is that 'in Christ' there is no longer anyone who can be considered an **alien** or a **stranger.** Paul moves back to talking of **you,** because this news is specially important for Gentiles.

> Consequently, you are no longer foreigners and aliens, but fellow citizens with God's people and members of God's household (2:19).

The situation recounted in verse 12 has been overcome. All the redeemed people of all nations are now **fellow citizens** with **God's people** (Greek: 'with the saints'). Recently my wife, after 35 years of living in England, took out British citizenship. This gives her all the same rights in law in the country that I have had ever since I was born. Paul's idea here is just this. Citizens have rights. Citizens under God's rule jointly share in the covenant promises, they are led by the same King, they share the great inheritance that belongs to **God's people**. It also means, as we shall see later, that they have responsibilities. In the past, Israel had many defined privileges in her special relationship with the Lord; these are now the possession of all God's people who are now defined as those who are part of the 'one body' in Christ.

In a pleasing addition to this idea of citizenship, Paul also uses the metaphor of a household or family. This helps us see the intimacy that there is to be among God's people. Having been strangers (literally 'away from home') we are now 'at home', with all its connotations of family, of safety, love, caring and warmth.

> built on the foundation of the apostles and prophets, with Christ Jesus himself as the chief cornerstone. In him the whole building is joined together and rises to become a holy temple in the Lord. And in him you too are being built together to become a dwelling in which God lives by his Spirit (2:20-22).

These Christians have, as it were, been drawn into a building being formed by God. No doubt this happened as they were converted and came to faith in Christ. The picture may remind us of 1 Peter 2:5 where God's people are called 'living stones'. The **chief cornerstone** is, of course, Jesus. He is the stone of the **foundation** that makes the whole building possible. He gives it its direction and purpose. But also making the whole building possible are **the apostles and prophets**. Although there is some debate about whether Paul has in mind the Old or New Testament prophets, it is most likely here that he thinks of the New Testament prophets. (It is clear that it is they who are in mind in 3:5 and 4:11.) The apostolic teaching concerning Jesus, and the application and immediate focus given to that teaching by the prophets in the church, provided all that was necessary for salvation, for true faith in Christ. Ephesians 3:4-6 is helpful here:

> you will be able to understand my insight into the mystery of Christ, which was not made known to men in other generations as it has now been revealed by the Spirit to God's holy apostles and prophets ... that through the gospel the Gentiles are heirs together with Israel, members together of one body...

That first generation of apostles and prophets were the ones, as these verses make clear, who first heard the revelation of Christ and who were able to proclaim the revelation of how Jews and Gentiles alike might become *members of the same body* through participation in Christ and receiving his gospel. So Paul sums up the further privileges that we have as God's people. He again uses the phrase **in him**, then follows it with **in the Lord** and yet another **in him**.

Thinking of the unity he has already spoken of in 2:16-18 by talking of the **whole building** being **joined together**, Paul now goes on to say that the building **rises to become a holy temple in the Lord**.

Just as God is in Christ, so we find that this building which is **in the Lord** is the place where God chooses to dwell. The aim is that all God's people shall be a great sanctuary where the presence of God himself will be manifest. Of course, God's Holy Spirit indwells the individual believer (see 1 Cor. 6:19), but this picture is of a great growing building that, whilst made up of many individual stones, is the place where God chooses to be.

The privilege of being 'in Christ' therefore also includes the privilege of being part of the universal church and knowing that we are part of something world-wide and quite extraordinary. Whether Paul was contrasting the church with the temple at Jerusalem or, more likely, the temple of Artemis in Ephesus, matters little. The idea of God being limited to the inner part of a great building set in one place in one country for one group of people has entirely gone. The picture is of the extraordinary wonder of God's people who find themselves to be a place set apart for God and in which he chooses to live **by his Spirit** (literally *in the Spirit*).

All Christians need to share in the joy that Paul feels as he writes of these great truths and privileges that we have in Christ. This place where God dwells is growing. It will continue to grow numerically, in spiritual depth, and across the nations until Christ returns. And while this happens we find this to be the most wonderful home built firmly on a sure foundation. It is a place of great unity (**joined together**) and peace, and where the love of God in Christ is best experienced and known.

Summary of Chapter 2

It is not too much to say of this chapter of Ephesians that Paul has shown us something of the heart of God.

First, we have seen that it is a *heart of grace*. Paul is bowled over by this concept, just as we ought to be. He repeated twice for emphasis and out of sheer joy and enthusiasm: '*it is by grace, the grace of God, that you are saved.*' This grace is his godly favour directed towards sinful men and women.

Secondly, the heart of God is a *heart rich in mercy*. This, Paul has shown us, is the great expression of God's love for us (v. 4). The *blood of Christ* was involved in showing this mercy. What astounding mercy it is that has led to our forgiveness and our acceptance as God's people in whom he dwells by his Spirit.

Finally, the heart of God is a *heart which always draws people to himself* in gracious forgiveness and acceptance. Reading that those *who once were far away have been brought near through the blood of Christ* ought to send a chill down the spine of all of us who are Gentiles. How wonderful is the inclusivity of the gospel and how beautiful this heart of God to draw even us to himself. Paul does not say God has made it possible but that we must now climb up to him to take advantage of it. He says it has happened for us 'in Christ', in whom we also find our unity. Together 'in Christ' Jews and Gentiles are fellow citizens in God's household. What more could we ask than to know that we are being drawn together as a dwelling in which God lives by his Spirit!

Further Application

First, we need to recognise that we live in an age which is massively preoccupied with achievement and self-interest. This chapter challenges many of the age's assumptions. The strongest possible emphasis is laid by Paul on God's grace. The heart of the gospel itself faces squarely all human assumptions about how clever or wise we may be. It refuses to allow that we have anything to do with our own salvation. Rather than us being the focus, God is the focus and it is vital that in all our talk of the Christian faith and in all our desire to serve the Lord we remember that that is always where our focus must be. God has achieved all this for us *in Christ*. We cannot and must not claim credit at any point, because to do so is to deny the gospel, however attractive it may be to people living in our generation. This humble focus on God and on Christ rather than on ourselves will also be attractive to those who are not of the faith. This is what it is to be 'Gospel People'.

Secondly, we must acknowledge that we live in a very individualistic generation. This passage reminds us of the worldwide family of God that is united through the redeeming work of Christ. Ethnic and geographical boundaries are broken down as the dividing walls of hostility are to be dismantled. All who are in Christ have the same privileges as God's family and his children. There is no distinction and we should seek to model that unity and interdependence much more clearly than we often do. We are *one body*, and this should make a difference. Locally, we should work at sharing our unity in Christ and love for each other. Internationally, we should be far more committed to help and pray for other Christians. We must get rid of any suggestion of superiority or of paternalism in our dealings with others, rather recognising how much we yet have to learn from Christians in other countries and with different experiences.

Thirdly, there is the matter of good works. There are times when I feel I am completely ruled by my diary. I keep it on one of those 'palm' gadgets. Each morning and evening I synchronise it with the diary my assistant has on her computer and she keeps an eye on me and points me in the right direction. But there are many times when I wonder where God is in all this. Life can be so busy. And some of my diary may well not be what God wants of me. This time pressure can also be present in all our church activities. But the wonder of what we found in 2:10, is that, assuming we are genuinely seeking to do what the Lord wants us to do, assuming that we are living in Christ, then we are assured that God has that diary under his control. We should be able to say the same of our church activities, but so often we fail in church life properly to seek out those works God has planned for us, preferring instead our man-made activities.

Fourthly, the lives we live now that we are 'in Christ' are to be lived as wholehearted and 'whole-bodied' responses to the amazing outpouring of God's love and mercy and grace to us who were once far away. God indwells us by his Spirit to enable us to do just that, yet still so many of us these days say something like this: 'I can't really do anything for the Lord', or 'I'm no good', or 'I'm not like that wonderful Christian'. Unfortunately this seems to ignore the whole teaching in this chapter about grace and love but also about the gracious good works that God has prepared for his people. We need to remind ourselves that once we are 'in Christ' there is indeed *significance in who we are*.

This truth is so important for our day and age. So many Christians feel they are no good to anyone, and certainly not to God. Men and women, young and old, feel they are worthless, and very little seems to change between before they were a Christian and after they have committed their life to the Lord. They are grateful to the Lord that he died for them and that they are now saved, but they still have such a low view of what may now be expected of God's people. Of course, we need to insist from this passage that any boasting is out. Some Christians really need to hear that. Yet there are other Christians who continue to deny that they are anybody. Paul is saying that 'in Christ' we *do* have significance. In fact, if it is sinful to boast, it must also be sinful to deny this great truth – 'You are God's workmanship.' If this is true then we

surely dare not say, 'I am worthless,' when it is God who
has made us. We dare not say to our Creator, 'You created
something worthless.' Paul says we are Christ's workmanship
and so, amazingly, we can achieve things for God. But there
is more, for Paul shows also that there is *significance in what
we do*.

Think of this! The Almighty God who saves us by his grace
does not *need* you and me to do anything at all for him, but
in his amazing grace he involves his people in his purposes
and plans. He *uses* even us. Sometimes as Christians we think
that God does not use us in the manner he uses someone else.
Perhaps we constantly compare ourselves with other people
and, in our opinion, we are always the loser. In our society of
competition, this is what so often happens. But what are we
saying to God, if we say something like this: 'God, I know
I am your workmanship, and I know you created me in Christ
Jesus to do good works. But you have made a mistake with
me'?

Through his apostle Paul, God speaks to our generation
and says, 'I am not comparing you with anyone, for I have
chosen you and loved you, I have redeemed you, and you are
my workmanship. In me you have your identity. Don't rely on
your friends or those around you, for I have loved you.'

Personally, I find this teaching extraordinarily moving.
After the facts of salvation themselves, surely this is one of the
most wonderful truths and blessings we could possibly have
'in Christ', that the Almighty God should have a use for us!
That the Almighty God should stoop, should condescend, to
involve me in bringing glory to him and to his name, is almost
beyond imagination. Isn't God gracious?

6

The extraordinary gospel revelation made to Paul
(Ephesians 3:1-13)

The start of this chapter reads rather strangely.

> For this reason I, Paul, the prisoner of Christ Jesus for the sake of you Gentiles (3:1).

Paul is about to write of how he is praying for the Ephesian Christians, but he is then diverted in his thinking and will only return to do so from verse 14 onwards.[1] The digression centres on Paul's calling to the Gentiles. Paul reminds his readers that he is in prison because he has been fulfilling Christ's calling that sent him to the **Gentiles**, and it is reflection on this that gives rise to the digression. **For this reason** looks back over Paul's whole exposition of the *mystery* of the faith and the privileges that all have who are *in Christ*, and we shall return to that when we look at verse 14.

Paul is a **prisoner** because he has followed Christ's call to go to the Gentiles. Paul belongs to Christ and will follow him wherever it leads as he seeks to obey the command to take the gospel to the nations of the world. Where Paul was in prison is debated but most agree that it was most likely in Rome. His way of expressing himself here stands as a challenge to all Christians. In prison at the hands of a cruel emperor,

---

1 Verse 14 begins '*For this reason...*'

Nero (54–68), Paul talks of being a prisoner **of Christ Jesus**. Whatever happens to him, however uncomfortable, however persecuted, Paul's commitment is to be Christ's *servant* (v. 7), and he therefore lives out what it really meant when Jesus said to his early disciples, 'If anyone would come after me, he must deny himself and take up his cross daily and follow me' (Luke 9:23).

> Surely you have heard about the administration of God's grace that was given to me for you, that is, the mystery made known to me by revelation, as I have already written briefly. In reading this, then, you will be able to understand my insight into the mystery of Christ, which was not made known to men in other generations as it has now been revealed by the Spirit to God's holy apostles and prophets. This mystery is that through the gospel the Gentiles are heirs together with Israel, members together of one body, and sharers together in the promise in Christ Jesus (3:2-6).

a) God's grace for Paul (3:2-3)

Paul starts by reminding the Ephesians that his calling was particular. He had the privilege and task of *stewarding* (administering) God's gracious gospel to them, the Gentiles. Paul had been given God's grace himself (see v. 8) with a view to bringing that grace to the Gentiles. So important was this calling that it still filled his mind and purpose even as he languished in prison in Rome. The grace of which Paul speaks is equivalent to **the mystery**. Paul probably has in mind his own amazing experience of God's grace to him on the Damascus Road as the time when things all fell into place for him and he came to understand that the truth of Christ was for all people. Paul has **already written** about this in 1:9-10 and in chapter 2. And so Paul's writing is itself designed to help them **understand** his gospel, what Paul calls **my insight**. This insight **has now been revealed by the Spirit to God's holy apostles and prophets**.

The message of the mystery, the revelation, is indeed something new. It was a revelation that had come from **the** *holy* **Spirit**. And it had come, as we saw earlier in 2:20, to the apostle Paul and to the other *apostles* and to the (New Testament) *prophets* who worked closely with the apostles.

b) The mystery revealed to Paul (3:4-6)

We have already seen the content of the **mystery** as we looked at 1:9. But here it is made very clear again that, for Paul, the inclusion of the Gentiles is at the heart of the whole revelation they have received: **through the gospel the Gentiles are heirs together with Israel**. It is this that is specially new, that **in Christ Jesus** all can be **sharers together in the promise**. The gospel is, above all, good news for those who were formerly never going to inherit the great covenant blessings that God had promised to his people. As in 2:5-6, here Paul thinks of the great privileges that even the Gentiles have **in Christ Jesus** and uses still more verbs with the Greek prefix meaning 'together with'. Here he talks of the Gentiles as **heirs together with Israel**, **members together** ('with Israel' is understood), and **sharers together** ('with Israel') in the promise **in Christ Jesus**.

c) God's power at work in Paul (3:7-12)

> I became a servant of this gospel by the gift of God's grace given me through the working of his power. Although I am less than the least of all God's people, this grace was given me: to preach to the Gentiles the unsearchable riches of Christ, and to make plain to everyone the administration of this mystery, which for ages past was kept hidden in God, who created all things (3:7-9).

Paul had come to faith entirely by grace, but here he has in mind the **gift of God's grace** which had prepared him and enabled him **to preach to the Gentiles**. When speaking of God's **power** enabling him to become **a servant of this gospel** Paul probably has in mind the specific enabling power of the Holy Spirit. He is describing here the *good works* which God had *prepared in advance* for the apostle himself to follow (2:10). Paul is supremely aware of what a work of power this had been. Not only had he experienced the power and glory of the

Lord on the road to Damascus, but he also knew what power had been at work in him to transform him from a persecutor of Christians and a 'Pharisee of the Pharisees' to one who saw it as vital that the whole world should hear of the love and forgiveness of God in Christ Jesus.

All Christians who think they could never be used of God should recall Paul's testimony here. He calls himself **less than the least of all God's people**, yet even so God's grace has worked powerfully in him so that he can be a vital preacher to the Gentiles. This grace enabled him to leave behind his old ways of thinking, his cultural and ethnic prejudices, to leave his home and his own people and go to the world as **a servant**. Paul is not being falsely humble here. Rather he reflects the inevitable reaction of one who has experienced the extraordinary power of saving grace but who also knows the enabling grace of God at work in his life. As Paul thinks of all that is inherited by those who are 'in Christ', he knows that nothing can compare with **the unsearchable riches of Christ**.

We have noted the nature of the *mystery* earlier. In 1:8-10 Paul has extolled God's love and wisdom for his people, which is to *unite all things in him*. But Paul's job in preaching is to make sure the wisdom and purposes of God are made known to all. Thus he is to preach these **unsearchable riches of Christ** to all indiscriminately. He is **to make plain to everyone** the content of the gospel and how God's purposes work and come together (**the administration**). Once again he refers to the fact that this was once known only to God, the God who **created all things**. This reinforces just how amazing is the power at work in Paul that has changed such a person so that he can be used in the service of the great creator God himself.

d) God's intention in revealing the mystery (3:10-12)
While human beings may have only come to understand the gospel through the apostles and prophets, that is not to say it was also new for God! Having talked of God as **creator of all things**, Paul once again establishes that it was always God's plan and purpose (see 1:4) to bring into being his church.

His intent was that now, through the church, the manifold wisdom of God should be made known to the rulers and authorities in the heavenly realms, according to his eternal purpose which he accomplished in Christ Jesus our Lord. In him and through faith in him we may approach God with freedom and confidence (3:10-12).

Now, that is, since the coming into being of the church in Christ, the church itself has been given a very important role in God's revelation. In the coming together of Jew and Gentile in one family, the church makes known **the manifold wisdom of God**. The fact of the existence of the church demonstrates categorically that God's plan has come into being and is being worked out. The church of Jew and Gentile, of people saved through faith in Christ from all over the world, stands as a clear and truly visual statement of God's mighty purposes. Paul says that these purposes of God are **made known through the church** to **the rulers and authorities in the heavenly realms**. For the meaning of *heavenly realms*, see comments on 1:3 and 2:6. However, here the description is not of the place where Christ is seated and Christians with him, but of the place where Satan dwells. As in 6:10, **the rulers and authorities** are those that are opposed to God and his purposes.

It is crucial to understand just how significant this work of God (**now**) through the church really is. In Old Testament times Israel had had a special covenantal relationship with God. They had frequently rebelled and sinned, but God had revealed himself in special ways to that nation alone. The Gentiles were very much under earthly rulers and authorities who reflected the rulers and authorities of Satan's realm. For example, the Pharaoh in the times of Moses is seen to be 'anti-God'. He represents on earth the forces that were always set against God rescuing, saving and redeeming his people. The existence of the church *which now includes Gentiles* is therefore a clear demonstration that Satan's plans have been foiled by God, and that God's eternal purposes are being worked out in spite of all that the rulers and authorities can do to oppose them.[2]

---

2 A few commentators believe that Paul refers here to the 'good' heavenly authorities – angels and the like. In the light of Paul's general argument and of 6:10 we have taken these authorities to be evil rulers.

Far too often in today's world we see 'church' as the place we go to worship on a Sunday. Even if we have a broader view than this, we often see it simply as 'the family of God around the world'. Paul here shows us how immense is the significance of the existence of the church because it finally reveals to Satan the long-term plans of God, plans that Satan's rulers and authorities had never understood until the establishment of the church. The church, then, speaks constantly to Satan and his cohorts demonstrating to them that they have not been able to stop the progress of God's plans. In Christ, on the cross, they were defeated (**which he accomplished in Christ Jesus our Lord**). Though that defeat of Satan and his forces is complete, their total subjugation to **Christ Jesus our Lord** will happen when Christ returns to judge. Meanwhile the church serves as a constant reminder to everyone that Satan and evil is defeated and that God's rule extends to all people, and Christ is indeed Lord.

It is for this reason that it is important for us all to realise that what the church looks like *does* matter. It should reflect the transcultural, transethnic unity that is part of God's plan. The more clearly we reflect this the more clearly we proclaim to the world and to the evil powers the victory of our Lord Jesus Christ.

One of the clearest ways the church proclaims the victory of Christ is that **in him and through faith in him we may approach God with freedom and confidence** (v. 12; see comments on 2:18). Nothing is able to stand in the way of our access to God if we are in Christ. The church is no longer in bondage to Satan but can come to the Father **with freedom**. Its **confidence** in doing this rests entirely on the work of Christ, hence **in him** and **through faith in him**.

e) Paul's sufferings (3:13)

Paul has described the joy of his calling and the message that he must preach, but it is delivered at a cost. Two ages, as it were, overlap. This is the age of the church, the age of salvation and redemption, the age in which Christ's victory is being proclaimed. But it is not yet the future age, the age when the fullness of God's purposes will have been finally worked out. Thus the church exists side by side with those serving the evil rulers and authorities. Sometimes it will seem that they are winning, though such is, in reality, certainly not true. Paul remains in prison and he has suffered much at the hands of persecutors. Ephesian Christians were concerned for him and so he adds:

> I ask you, therefore, not to be discouraged because of my sufferings for you, which are your glory (3:13).

Paul knows that the victory is Christ's, come what may. He knows that there is no need **to be discouraged** at apparent setbacks such as his imprisonment and **sufferings**. The word Paul uses here for *sufferings* is often used to describe especially those sufferings that characterise this age for the followers of Christ. They are the result of witnessing for Christ in this period but, in themselves, become a reminder that Christ will return. Jesus himself uses the word as he talks about how this age relates to the next in, for example, Matthew 24:9: 'Then you will be handed over *to be persecuted* [literally 'to sufferings'] and put to death, and you will be hated by all nations because of me.'[3]

For Paul there can be no discouragement as long as the message of the gospel is being carried to the Gentiles. Much the opposite. Paul's sufferings are evidence that the gospel is indeed being carried to the Gentiles and that God's purposes in Christ are being brought to fruition. This is their **glory** that they too as Gentiles may be for *the praise of his glory* (1:14).

So Paul brings to an end this digression that began with 3:2. By talking of the gracious and wonderful calling that God has given him, Paul has developed further his own role in preaching the mystery that is now revealed. He has spoken more fully of the importance of this revelation coming to the Gentiles, and how the church that is formed from the coming together of Jew and Gentile speaks of Christ's victory over

---

3 See also Matthew 24:21, 29; Mark 13:19, 24 and John 16:33: 'I have told you these things, so that in me you may have peace. In this world you will have trouble [literally 'suffering']. But take heart! I have overcome the world.'

Satan. But he has also enabled the Ephesian Christians to see that, therefore, his imprisonment is not something to cause despair or discouragement but rather it is, itself, evidence of the power of the gospel. In the apparent weakness of Paul as a person, in the apparent weakness of his position in prison, there is evidence that God's purposes are being fulfilled. The Gentiles are being reached, the sufferings promised by Jesus as a mark of the end times are being experienced. History is marching on under God's purposes towards its final destiny when Christ the Lord will return and the reality of the unity of God's people and their peace with God will be seen by all.

7

Paul's second prayer for the Ephesian church
(Ephesians 3:14-21)

The high calling of the church to reveal the mystery of God's purposes to the world and to the rulers and authorities will need great strength of purpose. More than that, church members will need to be strengthened inwardly if they are to face the hard work involved in this and the sufferings and persecutions that will come their way. Nothing will be more important to this church than that all its members have a truly deep grasp of the wondrous love of God in Christ that is directed towards them constantly, whatever their circumstances. It is this that Paul has grasped in all its depth as he languishes in prison. It is this that is now the substance of his prayer for the Ephesians. So Paul returns to his prayer.

> For this reason I kneel before the Father, from whom his whole family in heaven and on earth derives its name (3:14-15)

For this reason picks up on 3:1. It is because of all that has happened in Christ and through God's love that Paul has a special prayer for these people.

a) Prayer to the Father (3:14-15)
Paul refers to God as **Father** many times in his writing. There is little doubt that this was the practice of most early Christians, following Jesus' own teaching about how to pray in what we call 'The Lord's Prayer' (see Matt. 6:9). **[f]rom whom his whole**

family may better be translated as *from whom every family ...* or *from whom all fatherhood in heaven and on earth is named.*[1] Paul here stresses both the honour and reverence afforded to the Father as he **kneels**.

But Paul has more to say about the Father. Paul is praying to the one who has the power to answer because he is the creator of all fatherhood or of every family. Every **family in heaven and on earth derives its name** from him. This God is over all creatures, whether in the heavenlies or on earth, and so he will hear and be interested as Paul prays for this particular family grouping of Ephesian Christians. Yet, more than that, he will be able to answer the prayer because he is the *creator* **Father**. So Paul describes his prayer for these people in verses 16 to 19.

It is a prayer for the power of God to fill them so they may become mature in their inner being, knowing the indwelling presence of Christ, thus being filled to all the fullness of God.

> I pray that out of his glorious riches he may strengthen you with power through his Spirit in your inner being, so that Christ may dwell in your hearts through faith. And I pray that you, being rooted and established in love, may have power, together with all the saints, to grasp how wide and long and high and deep is the love of Christ, and to know this love that surpasses knowledge – that you may be filled to the measure of all the fullness of God (3:16-19).

In 1:18-19 Paul had prayed that their hearts would be opened to see the riches that are theirs in Christ. Knowing those riches was to know also *his incomparably great power for us who believe*. This, Paul had said, was the same power that had raised Jesus from the dead and exalted him in the heavenly realms (1:20). Paul still has this in mind here. He prays for their strengthening with **power**. The word *power* links this whole section together. Paul prays for it in verses 16 and 18 and refers again to God's

---

1 The significance that all *fatherhood* is from God should not be overlooked. In chapter 6 Paul will speak of fathers and children. God is to be imitated, and fatherhood reflecting the creator should receive much greater respect than it does in this day and age.

great power in the doxology of verse 20. This he knows comes about through the work of the Holy Spirit and it involves the **inner being** (meaning the same as the **heart** in v. 17). The end result will be one of being **filled** with **all the fullness of God**.

i) Prayer for strengthening power in the inner being (3:16-17)
Paul has spelled out the **riches** that we have in Christ in the first two chapters (see 1:7, 18; 2:7 also 3:8). Now he prays on bended knee **that out of his glorious riches** they may know God's **power** within them.

Paul had urged his readers not to be discouraged in verse 13. What he prays for is that they will realise what is theirs already through the Spirit of God. It is the **Spirit** who will **strengthen** them in their **inner being**. They need this power and strengthening to face this world in which they have to stand for Christ, a world in which they will sometimes feel powerless and alone, and certainly without any power in the world's eyes. Faced with the apparent power of Artemis and the sorcery or magic around them, Paul is aware that their greatest need is to know the reality of Christ's powerful presence with them even in the most adverse circumstances.

We must not separate the Spirit from Christ as if the Spirit were somehow an impersonal force that gives power. Rather it is by the powerful work of the Holy Spirit that Christ is known in the innermost part of the Christian's being. This indwelling of Christ by his Spirit in the life of the believer is essential for our comfort in difficulties, but also for power to live as we should for him, to witness for the gospel, and conduct our lives in a holy way reflecting Christ himself.

Verse 17 speaks of the same thing. This indwelling of Christ at the very heart of our being is appropriated **through faith**. As we place our faith in the one who died for us and brings us forgiveness of our sins, so we find him taking up residence at the centre of our lives by his Spirit. Sometimes Christians will talk of 'inviting Christ into my life' when they think of first becoming a Christian and placing their faith in him. Here, though, Paul is praying that the reality of this presence of Christ in the believer's life may have a dramatic effect on the life of the believer. He is concerned with the *continuing* impact of the Spirit's presence, that is, the continuing impact of the indwelling of Christ. As we shall see below, the aim of this prayer is that Christians may become more and more like Christ himself. As Calvin put it: 'Christ is not to be viewed from afar by faith but to be received by the embrace of our minds, so that He may dwell in us, and so it is that we are filled with the Spirit of God.'[2]

ii) Prayer for the ability to grasp the love of Christ (3:17-18)

Paul continues, (literally) *so that you* **being rooted and established in love, may have power ... to grasp ...**With Christ indwelling the believer by the power of the Holy Spirit, the person's life will undoubtedly be rooted and grounded **in love**. The presence of Christ brings the extraordinary love of God right to the centre of our being, for although that love of God is the source of our salvation, it is also the basis on which we are enabled to move forward in this world as disciples of Christ. This is why it is so vital that we **grasp** the full extent (**how wide and long and high and deep**) of **the love of Christ**.[3] The idea Paul has in mind is something like this: Through faith we receive the love of God as Christ dwells in our inner being by the power of the Spirit. By this same Spirit we receive power to grasp and experience this love that indwells us, and thus to grasp its implications for our lives. Thus we shall lead lives that will be stronger and more powerful in witness and holiness and in the demonstration of love. But we shall also live lives that are less discouraged (v. 13), and that are full of worship and praise to the one who has so loved us (vv. 20-21).

Thus far we have seen that Paul's prayer can be applied to the individual believer, but we must be aware that this is his prayer *for the church*. This comes out again in the words **together with all the saints**. It is not even just the Ephesian Christians who must grasp the wonder of Christ's love, but all Christians

---

2 J. Calvin, *Ephesians*, 168.

3 *The love of Christ* has been added at the end of verse 18. In Greek we read '... and high and deep, and to know (v. 19)...'. The NIV addition captures the right meaning.

across all ages. While all that is said applies to the individual believer, its importance for the church must not be missed. Together as God's people, members of his family, we grasp the full extent of God's love in Christ. As we saw in 2:22, God lives by his Spirit in his church, that is, among his people. Each individual has the Spirit of Christ within, but each individual is part of the body in which Christ dwells and in which his love is experienced and seen. This is clearly evidenced as the gospel of Christ reaches out to the Gentiles and to the whole world. There are no geographical or racial boundaries to this love of God. It even extends through persecution and death. Once again, knowing this love requires the **power** of the Spirit, and this leads to the climax of his prayer for the church at Ephesus.

iii) Prayer that they may be filled to the fullness of God (3:19)
On the one hand Paul prays that we may **grasp** the amazing love of Christ, and yet he knows too that, ultimately, this is a life-long endeavour for God's people and one that cannot ever be satisfied until we see him face to face, for we are **to know this love that surpasses knowledge.** There is no way in which the real depth of God's love in Christ can be grasped by fallible human beings. Indeed, anything that we might grasp of God's love will only be by the power of the indwelling Spirit of Christ. Yet even so, the growing and maturing in understanding and experience of that love is something that no Christian should ignore, for it truly roots us and establishes us in Christ himself. Thus, the climax is reached in an extraordinary statement: **that you may be filled to the measure of all the fullness of God**. This is the goal of Christians. It can also be described as becoming Christ-like (see 4:13). Our goal as individuals and supremely as the church, the body of Christ, is fully to reflect the image of God (see comments on 1:23). As we come to know and experience the wonder of Christ's love at work deep within us, so we will go on and on being filled with the Spirit (5:18).

The progression in Paul's prayer here is interesting. In line with Christ's words in John's Gospel (14:26; 15:26; 16:15), the Spirit points us to Christ and so Paul first asks that the Spirit will empower us to grasp the extraordinary love of Christ. No doubt as we grasp this it will be centred in our amazement that he should die for us to bring us grace and mercy and reconciliation. But as we come to Jesus and grasp more and more deeply this love that **surpasses knowledge** so we come to God himself. This prayer is profoundly Trinitarian. No wonder Paul moves now to doxology and praise as he commends this church to God.

b) Prayer to God whose power is at work in his people (3:20-21)

In what follows we are reminded of 1:19 where Paul had prayed that these Christians would know God's *incomparably great power for us who believe*. There he had made that remarkable statement that this power at work in the Christian is the same power that brought Jesus to life and *seated him in the heavenly realms*. Paul is still thinking along these lines.

> Now to him who is able to do immeasurably more than all we ask or imagine, according to his power that is at work within us, to him be glory in the church and in Christ Jesus throughout all generations, for ever and ever! Amen. (3:20-21)

Just as we cannot hope to grasp fully the love that surpasses knowledge, so we cannot imagine how great is the power of God at work in his people. The tragedy is that because we so fail to **imagine** it, so we fail to **ask** for it. For Paul this understanding of God's power is not a theological nicety; rather it is profoundly vital to the Christian life, and we sense the deep emotion as the apostle writes. How often Paul had had to rely on the power of God throughout his life: power to withstand temptation, power to stand firm when persecuted, power to preach when feeling weak, power to persevere in all types of trials. Paul knew God at work within him. The praise of God's people is thus directed to the one **who is able to do**. God can think and do and speak and work where we so often fail. And as we commit ourselves to this God and bring him **glory**, so we find his power is **immeasurably more than all we ask or imagine** and that it is at work within us, because his

Spirit dwells in our inner being (we were reminded in v. 16), and because Christ dwells in our hearts (v. 17).

The *glory* to be rendered to God has to do with recounting back to God the wonder of his nature. He alone has all 'glory'. The word effectively summarises all that is true of God himself. It has to do with his perfection, his light, his splendour, his wisdom, his power and so much more. The *glory* of God is precisely all that belongs to him. We easily understand that this glory is revealed **in Christ Jesus**. In Hebrews 1:3 we read: 'The Son is the radiance of God's *glory* and the exact representation of his being.' We remember also John 1:14: 'The Word became flesh and made his dwelling among us. We have seen his *glory*, the *glory* of the One and Only, who came from the Father, full of grace and truth.' That glory is brought to the Father through the Son is without question for Christians. What is the more unexpected, however, is that this glory is also to be found **in the church**. But this brings us right back to the prayer of the last few verses. The fact of the matter is that the more Christ's love is known and experienced in the inner being of Christians, the more they will reflect Christ himself, and the more they do that, the more they bring glory to God, reflecting back to him that which is entirely of him.

While individuals can and do bring glory to God in what they do and say and in how they think as they seek to imitate Christ, Paul's deepest concern here is to help us understand the nature of the church itself. As believing people make up the church, so the church in her worship and life reflects the beauty of the bride adorned for her husband (Rev. 21:2). As the church follows Christ more and more closely and prepares for his second coming, so she reflects something of his glory. As John puts it in Revelation 19:7: 'Let us rejoice and be glad and give him glory! For the wedding of the Lamb has come, and his bride has made herself ready.'

Paul looks forward to that perfection of the glory of the church in 5:27, but even now this is her great duty, to reflect all that is true of the perfection of our God, and thus constantly to be pointing beyond herself to him. And this is how it is to be **throughout all generations, for ever and ever!**

All this will happen as Christ lives in us and as we acknowledge the great depth of the love that we experience in Christ. It will happen to the extent that the power of the Spirit works within us to enable us to grasp hold of that love and to live it out in obedience and self-sacrifice. This great doxology thus moves seamlessly into chapter 4 as Paul talks about our great calling and how we are to work it out. This is a calling to reflect the image and glory of Christ and of God, a calling which depends on the power of the Spirit at work in us to enable us to do immeasurably more than all we ask or imagine.

Summary of Chapter 3

The apostle has spoken first, of his own wonderful calling by God to take the gospel to the Gentiles. Because of his submission to this calling he is in prison. His very special calling is of extraordinary importance to the Ephesians and all subsequent generations, for he is to proclaim the amazing truth that Gentiles who believe in Christ, as well as believing Jews, are 'sharers together in the promise of Jesus Christ'.

With deep concern for those to whom he writes, Paul explains that his sufferings should not discourage them. They reflect the fact that Christ is being honoured and the gospel being preached 'for the praise of his glory'. So he urges them not to lose heart and then explains how he prays for them.

Above all, he prays that they would be encouraged and strengthened in the inner person, that Christ may truly dwell in them, and that they may know the vast extent of the love of Christ.

Further Application

This chapter has profound implications for the modern church and how it lives and behaves. A few points worth considering are listed below.

Firstly, we must always remember the mission to the Gentiles. Paul has stressed his particular role in this mission. His role in the spread of the Gospel is continued by the church. One of the great sadnesses of the church today is that she has often lost the heart for mission. Paul makes it clear that this mission has always been fraught with difficulties and has even led to persecution. Such remains true today as we live in 'these last days'. This should not in any sense make us despair or give up as we look at the dark world around us. Rather we should see the very difficulties, sufferings and persecutions as part of an indication that we are doing what Christ wants us to do, and that these last days are upon us. It is the church's duty, and therefore our individual duty, to be part of the body of Christ which makes known the wisdom of God to the authorities and powers of this world and to all who, at the moment, are slaves to other lords. The urgency of this mission remains with us today and we need to ask ourselves what we are doing personally and how we are encouraging our church to get involved in such mission. Are we involved or do we simply give money to others to do the job for us?

Secondly, we need to recognise that we cannot live our Christian lives on our own. So often we believe that we can do things without God's help. Paul prays that we may be strengthened with power in our inner being. Recognising that God, in his grace, has given us great power through his Spirit, is part and parcel of developing a witnessing Christian life. It is vital that we understand that this power is given so that we may withstand temptations in the world, so that we may better bring glory to Christ, and so that we may withstand persecution as we witness for Christ. Many churches and many individual Christians seem to be powerless rather than powerful. It is all too easy to speak despairingly of our world or to feel that we can have no affect. But this passage encourages us to believe otherwise. We may not always see the effect of our witness for Christ, and we may not always see numbers come to faith as the church carries out its mission, but we do know that we can go out in the power of God and for his name's sake.

Thirdly, we need to recognise how amazing is Christ's love for his people. We should so recognise this love and long for it that we find ourselves gradually becoming more and more Christlike. This love of Christ for us should be both our example but also the power within us that enables us to love God's people and to love those outside as we seek to bring them also to know this great love of God in Christ Jesus.

So often it seems that we are unable to demonstrate Christ's love among ourselves and perhaps this is because we fail to appreciate his love for us. The power of a church and its ministry, when that ministry is saturated in God's love, is something extraordinary to see. It undoubtedly encourages those who have no faith in Christ to look again at the message of the gospel, and it allows us to be more effective in day-to-day life as we seek to bring glory to God.

Living a Christian Life

(Ephesians 4–6)

Paul has talked about the great treasures that are ours in Christ. He has spoken of the wonders of God's grace in Christ; he has spoken of the calling of God's people from all nations of the world, Gentiles and Jews; he has prayed for the church's strengthening by the Holy Spirit and that the church and individual Christians would grasp the depths of the love of Christ. This led him again to praise God who can do so much for us and in us to his glory. It is thus no surprise that he now moves on to teach about how Christians should live if the church is truly to reflect God's glory to the world and indeed back to God and to reflect the love of Christ. Thus, even though chapter 4 seems to begin a second half of this letter, moving from the more doctrinal to more practical admonitions concerning the Christian life, the two halves are integrally tied together. It is because we have all this marvellous inheritance 'in Christ', that we should now consider how to respond in our lives.

Back in 2:2 and 2:10 Paul had used the word **walk** to describe the way people live. There he prepared the ground for these last three chapters. He had written in 2:2 of how these Ephesian Christians used to walk (NIV – live) when they followed Satan, and he had then mentioned the good works that God had prepared in **advance for us to walk in (2:10)**. The verb *'to walk' helps express the very active response* that is required of all Christians to the favours God has lavished upon them. This verb (translated as 'to live' in the NIV) leads us into five main sections as the apostle spells out how the church should behave in responding to the grace of God.

I

Walk in a manner worthy of the calling
(Ephesians 4:1-16)

As a prisoner for the Lord,[1] then, I urge you to live a life
worthy of the calling you have received (4:1).

If our calling is to reflect the image of God and bring him
glory at all times, to imitate Christ and reveal God's love
to the world, then we must live a life worthy of the calling
(literally, walk in the calling with *which* you were called see
on 2:2). The word in Greek for being 'called' reminds us
of the word for church – 'called out'. 'You' (plural), Paul is
saying, 'must *live* in a way that will reflect the grace (you have
received) by which you have been called.' The gift of God of
salvation *in Christ*, the indwelling love of God, the power of
the Spirit within, all point to the possibility of changed lives.
But changed lives must be lived out. For Paul this means that
even as a prisoner he is in the Lord and must do this. There
will be no excuses for this Ephesian church nor for individual
members. Whether in prison or free, the Lord must come first
and be the focus of the whole of life.

Leading a **worthy life** means doing the works in our lives
which arise out of God's grace and enabling *power*, for which
he has just prayed. They are *the good works which God prepared
in advance for us to walk in* (see on 2:10). So what will this life
look like? It will, of course, ultimately be one that reflects
Christ.

---

1 Greek 'in the Lord' rather than 'for the Lord' as in NIV.

a) Live in Unity (4:2-4)

Paul's first emphasis is that this life will be one that demonstrates unity.

> Be completely humble and gentle; be patient, bearing with one another in love. Make every effort to keep the unity of the Spirit through the bond of peace (4:2-3).

Verses 1-3 are all one sentence. Paul says **I urge you ... to live ...** being **completely humble and gentle**. These words further emphasise the imitation of Christ. In Philippians 2:8 Paul uses Christ as the model for our humility. Christ is also described as **gentle** as, for example, in Matthew 11:29: 'Take my yoke upon you and learn from me, for I am *gentle* and humble in heart, and you will find rest for your souls.'[2]

Gentleness in our relationships with others is the opposite of dominating or forcing ourselves on people. It is about consideration for the other, about peacefulness rather than provocation. The apostle Peter also refers to the beauty of such gentleness in the Christian life in 1 Peter 3:4: 'Instead, it should be that of your inner self, the unfading beauty of a *gentle* and quiet spirit, which is of great worth in God's sight.'

Humility means putting the other person first, thinking of his or her needs before our own. These qualities link directly with being **patient** and with **bearing with one another in love**. These virtues are absolutely essential and will require *great* **effort** if we are **to keep the unity of the Spirit through the bond of peace**. This unity is the unity that the church has in Christ. Here is where Jew and Gentile are to live together in peace. Here is where, as we shall see in chapters 5 and 6, slave will rub shoulders with master, where wife and husband and child and parent will worship together. Here is where they will be asked to work out a new model for living, one which is full of humility and patience and forbearance as the community seeks to live its life in the love of God and bonded together in the **peace** of God. They do not have to make this peace, for it

---

2 Also see Matthew 21:5: 'Say to the Daughter of Zion, "See, your king comes to you, *gentle* and riding on a donkey, on a colt, the foal of a donkey."'

has been established through the work of God 'in Christ' (see 2:14-17). Rather, the appeal is that they will behave towards each other (converted Jew and converted Gentile) in a way that will model the new order created in Christ.

It is worth remembering here that 'peace' was always one of the great blessings of the last days for which the prophets and people of Old Testament days longed. As Israel battled with her Gentile enemies and the true prophets spoke of God's judgement on his people through the wars, so false prophets said 'peace, peace' when there was none (Jer. 6:14). Yet God, in his sovereign purposes, would indeed bring peace between Jew and Gentile, but not in the way many had expected. The 'bond' of peace would not come about by forming international treaties with surrounding nations but through the work of Christ. The long-expected shalom, peace, of the great covenants would come to fruition in Christ. The joy and inheritance of covenant blessings for God's people always included 'peace', peace with God and peace between peoples. It was part of the gospel message itself in Isaiah 52:7. It was part of the covenant promised in Isaiah 54:10 and Ezekiel 37:26. This great promise is fulfilled in Christ for his people and they must now live as people at peace with each other.

There can be few more difficult areas for all of us who are Christians than this, to **keep the unity of the Spirit**. As we shall see below, this too is founded in the very character of God. If he is three persons and yet one, so those who reflect his image should reflect this also, plurality, yet unity. Sometimes people have believed that this can be achieved by creating a structural unity in joining churches together or by bringing denominations together. While this may often be a desirable end, there is something much more dynamic in what Paul asks of us than dealing with structures. We are to be so rooted and grounded in love (3:17) that such unity becomes almost instinctive. This will require great effort and much prayer. We shall have to work at this person by person as we interact with other Christians.

It is worth noting that love precedes unity here. It is when the prayer that we should be rooted and established in love has been answered and when we have better grasped the wonder of Christ's love, that we can move forward to love so much that unity is uppermost in our mind as we relate to brothers and sisters in Christ. Those of us in loving relationships know only too well how this works. If I have a disagreement or even, God forbid, an argument with my wife, it can never last long. I love her far too much to let the disagreement spill over for long. So it should be with others too. We should so love others that we are prepared to be humble and patient and forbearing with them, thus maintaining that unity that has as its core the Spirit's work in the church's life.

b) Theological background for unity (4:4-6)

There is one body and one Spirit – just as you were called to one hope when you were called – one Lord, one faith, one baptism; one God and Father of all, who is over all and through all and in all (4:4-6).

The seven-fold repetition of the word *one* drives home the theological basis for the requirement of unity. As we saw in 2:15-16 this unity that we are to work at is seen in God himself and also in his calling. For all our stress in the western world on individual faith and commitment, we have already seen how this epistle speaks to us as people who are part of God's worldwide church and described as **one body** (see 1:23). As Jew and Gentile are brought together through faith in Christ and hostility is broken down (2:11-14), so the church reflects that which is true of God himself. He is one, yet he is Father, Son and Spirit. Unity and diversity are there in the Godhead and so are to be part of what the church reflects in portraying the image of God.

Led by the **one Spirit**, the **one body** is **called to one hope**. We have seen the nature of this 'hope' back in 1:18-19a. Here it summarises the gospel itself. It looks forward to the time when God's full plan of salvation will be completed and Christ returns in glory. Meanwhile we remember that the **one Spirit** is the 'deposit' guaranteeing the fulfilment of God's purposes 'to the praise of his glory' (1:14).

The Lord Jesus is the **one Lord** and it is the teaching of Scripture that it is through faith in him alone that salvation may be found, hence there is **one faith** and **one baptism**. The title *Lord* is used sixteen times in these last three chapters of the epistle. Paul's exhortation to Christians to live lives worthy of their calling is based on the fact that Christ comes to his people, to his church, as the covenant Lord. He comes with the steadfast love of one who has made promises to his people that he will never rescind, but he also comes as the Lord who demands obedience and service. Thus, often in the apostle Paul's passages of ethical exhortation it is this title that he uses. In turning to Christ in **faith** the Ephesians have accepted the *word of truth, the gospel of [their] salvation* (1:13) and thus have committed themselves to his Lordship in their lives and the life of the church (1:15). The outward sign of this inward reality in the life of these believers is that they all undergo **one baptism**, baptism into the Lord Jesus Christ. Baptism would have been the place where all converts were asked to profess their faith in the **one Lord**.

The statement **one God and Father of all** brings this series of seven to a great climax. Ultimately, though the emphasis here is on **one**, these three verses make a magnificent Trinitarian statement. A question arises here as to whether Paul has in mind the Fatherhood of God over all Christians or over all people or over all the world. Since the **one body** and the **one faith** and **one Lord** all refer to the church, to Christians, it is often assumed that the same is true here. However, it is also possible, and probably more likely, that Paul has in mind God the Father's utter and total sovereignty over all things and all people. He continues with the statement **who is over all and through all and in all**. Paul makes a similar confession in 1 Corinthians 8:6: 'for us there is but one God, the Father, from whom all things came and for whom we live.' So what then is Paul saying?

The unity of the church under one Lord is a witness to the world concerning the one true God. The witness by people who have admitted to Christ's Lordship and who have come to the **one hope** and **one faith** is that there is just **one God** who has complete sovereignty over all. The phrase **through**

all and in all recalls the nature of God's immanence. He is active in all things to bring about his purposes to 'the praise of his glory'. He is the creator Father who calls upon all to turn to him in repentance and faith and who must be obeyed for he is **over all**. This is part of the church's confession and witness to the world. The unity demanded of the church is designed to proclaim to the world *one God*, Father, Son and Spirit who is to be worshipped by all who wish to find salvation.

Further Application

Paul's emphasis here on unity is a vital lesson for all ages but, perhaps especially, for ours. *First, we should be unified in our local churches.* The lack of perceived and of actual unity among believers worshipping in the same church brings dishonour upon God and flies in the face of his Spirit's work among us. Humility, patience and forbearing with each other are often not what most characterises church members. Paul insists this work takes *effort*. Biting our tongues may be essential. We must learn discernment so that we can judge whether it is essential for the sake of the gospel truth to indicate we differ from someone, or whether we simply differ because we have different tastes or backgrounds or preferences.

We cannot ignore the fact that in a post-modern age people are especially interested in how communities (like the church) function and whether they are genuine and trustworthy. Lack of unity therefore hinders the spread of the gospel, as well.

Secondly, the worldwide church should seek ever closer unity. If the theological reason for unity lies in the person of God himself, then we must struggle to witness to that unity in every possible way. While this is not fundamentally about structural or denominational unity, we should not ignore the quest for greater unity at this level. However, there are many ways we can reflect our unity more clearly than we do. In a world where so many people live in darkness and without hope in Christ, we can surely work better than we do towards a goal of unity. Often this is best seen in outreach and evangelism where we become concerned with the big matters of eternal life and death rather than the niceties of petty theological differences. I am excited when I see foreign missionaries standing side by side with national Christians helping in ways that are needed. I am depressed when I see missionaries setting up new, slightly different churches in towns where Bible-believing churches already exist; after all, there are so many towns in most nations with no Bible-believing, gospel-preaching churches at all.

c) The grace for unity (4:7-16)
None of our efforts towards unity or demonstrating the love of God that is ours in Christ is at all possible of our own, and so, Paul moves to describe the grace that we have been given to enable us to be this united people, this one body.

> But to each one of us grace has been given as Christ apportioned it (4:7).

Here we may recall chapter 2. Salvation is entirely of grace (2:5, 8), but notably for Paul's discussion here in chapter 4, the works prepared beforehand for us to *walk* in are also part of God's gracious work in his church and for his church (see 2:10 and 4:12). God's grace has **been given as Christ apportioned it**, not just to the special few, not just to each of the apostles, but **to each one of us**. This is, of course, part of being *one body*. Each member will have to be a working part for the body to function and to present itself as united and reflecting of the glory of God. As Paul makes clear in verses 11 and 12, he specially has in mind the way God gives grace gifts to his people so that they can minister to each other in a way that will build up the church *until we all reach unity in the faith and in the knowledge of the Son of God.*

As we have seen unity and differentiation in the Godhead, so we see it here in the church. The church is to be **one body** and united and yet it is made up of many individuals and **to each one of us grace has been given**. It is Christ's church and it is therefore he who apportions the **grace** necessary to achieve his purposes of bringing disparate people from many different backgrounds together under his Lordship, into one people who witness to him and the one true God. As we shall see, this grace is seen in a number of ways, but specially in the gifts that are given to enable the body to grow in its knowledge of Christ.

Paul now breaks off to appeal to ideas from Psalm 68 in an interesting and somewhat complex theological explanation of Christ's work on behalf of his church.[3]

> This is why it says: 'When he ascended on high, he led captives in his train and gave gifts to men.' (What does 'he ascended' mean except that he also descended to the lower, earthly regions? He who descended is the very one who ascended higher than all the heavens, in order to fill the whole universe) (4:8-10).

It says refers to Scripture. In Psalm 68:18 we read: 'When you ascended on high, you led captives in your train; you received gifts from men, even from the rebellious – that you, O LORD God, might dwell there.' In its original context this psalm of David praises God for going before the Israelites and defeating their enemies, bringing them out of Sinai, establishing them in Zion, and then providing for his people. The psalm praises God for his actions on behalf of his people. God, who abides *in his holy dwelling* is called *father to the fatherless* (v. 5). He leads his people and defeats their enemies. God's enemies flee as he reigns from *the mountain*, Zion (v. 16). He *led captives* in his train and *received gifts from men* (vv. 18, 29). The psalm itself is notoriously difficult to interpret, but the fact that Paul seems to change God's receiving of gifts to his *giving* of gifts makes it even more difficult for us to see what is going on. Neither is it particularly clear what the words **ascended** or **descended** refer to.

It may be that Paul did not intend this to be a direct quotation from Psalm 68:18 so much as an allusion to the whole psalm in which he recalls some words directly. The psalm, in line with Ephesians 4:6, praises God for his sovereignty over all things. Also it is important to see that the psalm is summarised in its last verse of praise with the fact that God, who reigns and

---

3 For a detailed analysis of some of the interpretative issues surrounding this text, see P.T. O'Brien *The Letter to the Ephesians* (Grand Rapids: Eerdmans, 1999).

has received gifts, *gives* gifts of power and strength to his people: 'You are awesome, O God, in your sanctuary; the God of Israel gives power and strength to his people. Praise be to God!' (v. 35). The grace gift of God's *power* has been much to the fore in Paul's thinking in 3:7, 16, 18, 20.

The ascension to which the psalm probably refers is to God leading the people from defeat of their enemies to his throne in Zion (perhaps recalling the ark which symbolised his presence among his people being taken to Jerusalem once Israel's enemies had been defeated). On his throne, God receives gifts from people (68:18), but he also dispenses power and strength to his people (68:35).

The New Testament regularly sees the Old Testament teaching about God being fulfilled in the King who is Christ, the Son of David. It is thus fairly straightforward for us to see that the ascension refers to Christ who, like the description of God in Psalm 68, has defeated his enemies and is exalted to his high throne. But to what does the 'descent' refer? The traditional understanding still seems to this writer to make the most sense. It is said to refer to Jesus coming in the incarnation and the start of his work on earth, which leads to the conquest of Satan in Jesus' death on the cross and then on to his exaltation. The order of descent–ascension in verse 10 suggests this is most likely. Christ **descended**, he came to this earth, defeated his enemies, and then **he ascended**. Having ascended, he then **gave gifts to men**. This giving of gifts would come with his gift of the Holy Spirit which followed the ascension.[4]

In spite of the very real difficulties of interpretation raised by Paul's use of Psalm 68, we may see that **Christ** (v. 7) is the one who has ascended and who has **apportioned** gifts, for he is the one **who ascended higher than all the heavens** (see 1:3, 20-21). It is surely truly humbling for us all that the one **who ascended higher than all the heavens, in order to fill the whole universe** should look on his people with such love

---

4 More recently some, like A. T. Lincoln, *Ephesians* (pp 243-44), have suggested that the ascent refers to the exaltation but the descent refers to the Spirit of Christ coming at Pentecost and bringing gifts.

and compassion that he should give us special grace gifts to enable us to serve him and grow to Christian maturity.

This great Lord is the one who provides the grace necessary for the church to be built up in such a way that its unity is shown forth. And he, Christ, is clearly the subject of the next sentence in verse 11.

c) The gifts necessary for unity (4:11-13)

> It was he who gave some to be apostles, some to be prophets, some to be evangelists, and some to be pastors and teachers, to prepare God's people for works of service, so that the body of Christ may be built up until we all reach unity in the faith and in the knowledge of the Son of God and become mature, attaining to the whole measure of the fullness of Christ (4:11-13).

Unity will be revealed as Christians mature in the faith and become increasingly Christ-like. As Paul had argued so carefully in 1 Corinthians 12, this means seeing that every member has a part to play and that the whole body sees itself as the body of Christ. But here Paul goes further and refers, as he does in Colossians 1:18 and 2:19, to Christ as the Head (of the body).

In his writings, Paul lists all sorts of gifts that Christ, by the Holy Spirit, has given to the church to enable it to grow and mature in the faith and by which members may build up the church. Though no list should be considered exhaustive, they can be found in 1 Corinthians 12 and 14, Romans 12 and in Ephesians 4. (In addition, Peter mentions some gifts in 1 Pet. 4.)

In verse 11 Paul picks up from where he had left off in verse 7. Christ had given grace **to each one**, but now he refers specifically to four groups of people who are part of Christ's gifts to his church. Each of the four have been given for their role in the ministry of the Word.

The first two are the **apostles** and the **prophets**. We discussed who these were as we looked at 2:20. These foundational ministries (which included the apostolic presentation and

Spirit-inspired interpretation of the revelation of Jesus Christ, and the prophetic application of this message) provided the basis for unity in the church. It was upon that early apostolic and prophetic proclamation of God's revealed truth, the truth of Christ, that the churches were planted and could gather and grow.

The next two are **evangelists** and **pastors.** Here we should probably also include **teachers** with pastors as the Greek construction suggests they should be regarded together. *Evangelists* went out with the apostolic and prophetic message to preach the gospel of Christ. Philip mentioned in Acts 6 and 7 stands as a notable example. He was a man who was described as *full of faith and of the Holy Spirit.* Along with six others he was originally chosen by the early church to help with problems of administration in the aid being given by the church to widows. In Acts 21:8 he is described as an *evangelist.* Timothy is also referred to as an *evangelist* in 2 Timothy 4:5. Both of these examples suggest that the gift of evangelist to the church is one that may be found among different types of church leaders. But the word itself reminds us that their work is to proclaim the evangel, the good news of Jesus Christ. Without such people the church might have grown deeper in its knowledge of Jesus but it would not have grown numerically and thus would have eventually died out. How much we should pray that, in his grace, Christ might give this gift generously to our churches today.

Pastors and teachers refer to the ongoing ministries so necessary to the well-being of the body of Christ. Christians need to be cared for pastorally and to be fed with teaching from God's Word. Such people are given to the church to ensure the care of God's people but also to ensure that they are held carefully within the bounds of apostolic, biblical truth. Pastors will lead people by feeding them on the Word, and caring for them and guiding them in their day to day lives. Both of these ministries look directly to Jesus as their inspiration. As Peter shows us in 1 Peter 5:1-4, Jesus is the Chief Shepherd on whom all other *pastors* or *shepherds* of God's people must model themselves. Teachers not only taught the facts of the faith but applied that truth to the lives of believers in the church, as we

see clearly in 4:21-23. They are also the ones who will offer
the first line of defence against those who would teach false
doctrine (4:14). Teachers also follow the example of Christ, the
Teacher, as they are expected to teach in word and by example
(John 13:13-15).

e) Working for unity (4:14-16)

Paul now writes that these gifts, that is, these apostles, prophets,
evangelists, pastors and teachers are given **to prepare God's
people**[5] **for works of service.** The idea here is that those
involved in laying the gospel foundations and in teaching
and applying God's Word are involved in instructing and
equipping **God's people** to fulfil their ultimate purpose and
goal. In the next two phrases Paul will spell out what this is.
However, the ultimate goal will only be achieved as everyone
in the church takes part in **works of service.** In verse 16 Paul
expands on this as he talks of *each part* of the body doing its
work towards the growth and unity of the whole. The goal is
now spelled out in two further clauses.

i) So that the body of Christ may be built up
It is worth taking a look back at 2:21-22 at this point. There we
read: *you too are being built together to become a dwelling in which
God lives by his Spirit.* In comments there we said that 'the
aim is that all God's people shall be a great sanctuary where
the presence of God himself will be manifest'. Paul has the
same picture in mind here. The church is a work in progress.
Different images are used to describe this – building, growing,
maturing – but all reflect the fact that the body of Christ is
a living organism that is becoming what God has created it to
be. Every Christian has a part to play in this work, and every
Christian is being prepared for his or her particular works
of service in that growing process by the contribution of the
pastors, teachers and others listed in verse 11.

ii) So that we may reach maturity
So Paul moves on to define further this goal and the purpose
of this work in progress. This work involves **we all**, that is all

---

5 Greek: 'The saints.'

Christians. And (v. 13) the work continues **until**... Paul now breaks this final sentence down into three parts. The structure looks like this: **until we all reach** – unity in faith; maturity; the measure of the fullness of Christ.

Although each of these elements do not mean the same thing, they combine together to help Christians understand what they are involved in and what they should be aiming at as members of the body of Christ. We have already seen the importance of **unity in the faith** in 4:3-6. As we saw in those verses, it is a unity founded in *one Lord, one baptism, one God and Father of all*. The focus of this unity is to be found **in the knowledge of the Son of God**. The same word for knowing was explained in 1:17 where Paul prayed that Christians might know the Father better. Paul had filled his Christian readers with joy as he listed, in chapter 1, all the treasures that are theirs 'in Christ'. Coming to know Christ in this context means to grow in our understanding of this inheritance and of all that Christ is and what he has done for us. It involves increasing, profound recognition of what was involved in redemption, appropriating more deeply the significance of God's work in Christ from before the foundation of the world, glorying in the joy of our inheritance, discovering ever more about the Lord, and seeking to spread the honour of his name in his world.

and become mature ('until we all reach ... maturity'). Maturity here is contrasted with what happens to *infants* in verse 14. The idea is of a grown man who is not easily moved around, but is firm in his conviction of the faith. However, we need to remember that this is not so much a picture of an individual mature Christian as a picture of the church itself. This is what **we all** are to reach, together. As we grow through our teachers and pastors, and study of the apostles and prophets in the Scriptures themselves, as we come to a deeper and deeper knowledge of the Son of God, so we shall mature in the one faith. We shall become more stable, less subject to doubt and confusion, and more able to live consistently for the Lord. Unity in faith and maturity thus go hand in hand. The maturer a church is in its knowledge of the Son of God, the more unified it will become.

attaining to the whole measure of the fullness of Christ ('until we all reach ... the fullness of Christ'). This is the final and most complete way of summarising the goal before us. It is to reflect Christ perfectly in the body of his church. (The discussion of 1:23 will help considerably in studying this clause.) We shall not finally reach this goal until Christ returns and the church is fully glorified, but this is what we are to be about. The church is ever more clearly to become the place where Christ and all his attributes and powers can be seen. As people look on the church, they should see Christ. They will not see this so much in each individual, but rather as the individuals all use their gifts together and so produce a unity that reflects the **fullness of Christ**.

This maturity is further expounded in the next three verses as Paul first contrasts the maturity of which he has been speaking with childhood (v. 14), and then paints a picture of that maturity (vv. 15-16).

> Then we will no longer be infants, tossed back and forth by the waves, and blown here and there by every wind of teaching and by the cunning and craftiness of men in their deceitful scheming. Instead, speaking the truth in love, we will in all things grow up into him who is the Head, that is, Christ. From him the whole body, joined and held together by every supporting ligament, grows and builds itself up in love, as each part does its work (4:14-16).

Paul talks of **we**, recognising that he too is as much part of this church and as much in need of hearing the warning as are those to whom he is writing. Different pictures are used to help make the point that **infants** are not mature and can easily be controlled and bounced around by other people. They are like sailing boats that can be **tossed back and forth by the waves** and **blown** anywhere the **wind** might take them. From the church's point of view maturity will be seen in how it responds to **teaching** and to the planned deception of those who wish to undermine the church. We have seen that unity is founded on the critical work of the apostles, prophets, and pastors and teachers. But the immature church may not take sufficient account of that vital teaching and instead listen to those who deceive in order to lead the church astray. The word **cunning** is used in 2 Corinthians 11:3 of the serpent, and it is the Devil that lies behind the **craftiness of men** who would deceive the church of Christ.

The danger for the modern church is as great as ever it was in the apostle's time. Those who have successfully divided the church in the past have almost always done this through deceit and cunning. They have not entered the church by the front door, as it were, so much as they have started to teach 'other teachings' (heterodoxy). They have often sounded reasonable and fair, even profound and good, but they have taken people away from the **fullness of Christ** to something that perverts the truth of who Christ is or what he has done. Thus we may think of those who, from within the church in our age, minimise or challenge the nature of Christ's substitutionary death on the cross or the complete trustworthiness of Scripture. How much more persuasive have been these attacks on orthodoxy than attacks that have come from blatant unbelievers outside the church!

The stark contrast between verse 14 and verse 15 helps us see the significance of the danger of immaturity and not taking the apostolic teaching seriously enough. The contrast between a people who remain as **infants** and a church which **grows up** into Christ, is one all readers will understand. An infant remains vulnerable to anyone who would hurt him. He needs constant feeding but will not know until it's too late whether he has been fed food that is good or bad. Infants are too young to discern what is right or wrong, and will be attracted by anything that makes them feel good.

Sadly, we live in an age where teaching and learning are often frowned upon and where church pastors, teachers and evangelists, in a desperate attempt to be 'contemporary' or 'relevant', fail to lead people deeper into the Word of God in Scripture, but rather emphasise only that which might make people feel good. Pastors seem often to treat the church entrusted to their charge as infants. Yet, instead of seeking to grow them into maturity in Christ, they speak down to their flock in a sort of childish talk that will never help people grow to face the temptations of this world or enable them to withstand the erroneous teachings of the **deceitful scheming** of the modern day heretic. Being tossed this way and that by any new teaching that might come along is contrasted with **speaking the truth in love,** and with coming to maturity.

Paul is clear that the **truth** must be spoken in **love.** This important clause has often been taken out of context. The words are often used as an excuse to tell others an upsetting or uncomfortable so-called 'truth' about themselves. 'I need to tell you this in love...' becomes a rather pious excuse for saying something mean or inconsiderate to another person. How different this use of the words is from Paul's intention in this passage. The apostle is determined we should understand the contrast not only between being infants or being mature but also between good teachers and pastors and others. Good teachers and pastors love the church in which God has placed them and work within the love of Christ. The crafty and cunning false teachers, who would lead people astray, do not *love* the people they are trying to influence because love, as it is taught in this epistle, will always point towards Christ and growth in him. This also explains why **truth** and **love** must never be separated in the church.

This separation of love and truth is commonplace and happens in all sorts of deceitful ways in the modern church. Many teachers will refuse to teach the more difficult and apparently less palatable parts of Scripture because they sound 'unloving'. Thus it is commonplace to find the teaching of God's justice and judgment omitted from the regular teaching of churches in some mistaken or deliberately deceitful view that the 'love' of God would prohibit his judgment. We find pastors refusing to speak against sexual sin or pride or materialism, because to do so would perhaps turn people away from the church. The excuse so often used is that we must above all show 'love' to all people. The problem with this argument is that it divorces love and truth in a way which never happens in Scripture. True love is seen in God's love and presenting this means telling the whole revealed counsel of God as it is found in Scripture. Indeed God's truth must be allowed to define our understanding of love.

The phrase **in love** has already been commented upon when it was used in 1:4, 3:17-18 and 4:2, and it will be used again in 4:16. Understanding the love of Christ was the subject of Paul's prayer in 3:14-19, and helps us see its significance here. Love has to do with the gospel and being 'in Christ', and with the plans of God for his people from before the foundation of the earth. As the gospel of Jesus Christ is proclaimed, so true love is proclaimed, God's love. Of course, we cannot divide this proclamation from living the life that is worthy of this calling to proclaim. That is the whole point of this section of the epistle. But love is so much more than simply communicating truth in a *nice* way! Sometimes the gospel will challenge in ways that upset and disturb. Sometimes the gospel will lead to lifestyles that are deeply counter-cultural, but they will still reflect real and true (God's) love to the extent that people are 'in Christ' and following him in word and deed.

It is precisely for this reason that it would be wrong to say that truth is ultimately more important than love or vice versa. The two are like different sides of the same coin. The revelation of God in Christ and of his saving purposes to the praise of his glory (as Paul has expounded it thus far in this letter) is the revelation of love and it is the revelation of truth. God's truth reveals his love which his people are to reflect. God's love reveals truth which his people are also to reflect in all they do and say. There can be no deception in the love of which Paul talks. Any reduction of the whole of God's revealed truth in Scripture would present a distortion of the fullness of God's love in Christ. Any lack of love or compassion or patience or forbearing in the presentation of truth would be a distortion of the fullness of God's truth in Christ.

Commitment to the gospel, the apostolic truth, commitment to the person of Christ as revealed by the apostles and taught by faithful pastors and teachers, is the God-given way of standing firm and is the God-given way in which his people **will in all things grow up into him who is the Head, that is, Christ**. This picture of Christ as **Head** builds on the body image of verse 12 and will be developed again in verse 16. Paul continues to develop his thoughts of verse 13: *become mature, attaining to the whole measure of the fullness of Christ*. The church's goal is to be built up in Christlikeness, and to reflect him in all that it is and does and speaks.

Becoming mature inevitably involves **the whole body** in growth, and this is led on by the power of the Holy Spirit who dwells within this building (see specially 2:22; also 1:17; 3:16; 4:3). Paul has highlighted the foundational and teaching and pastoring ministries earlier. He now sees these as the ministries by which the church is **joined and held together**. It is they, probably, rather than every member of the church, who are the **supporting ligament(s)**. But, naturally, the whole body is involved and so Paul returns to each individual member as he talks of **each part** doing **its work**. God's people live together and work together **in love**. That is, working out the truth of what it is to be in Christ and following the leading of the Spirit. And this is the purpose behind the command to live a life of unity.

As we have seen before in this epistle, the need to move beyond the individualism of our day and age and to see that the Lord puts before us a different model for existence in the church is a huge challenge for us. We are always tempted to go our own way or assume that we can grow in Christ on our own. How often do we hear from people that they are Christians but do not feel the need to go to church regularly! Yet just as serious a misunderstanding of the body of Christ is to be found among those who do go to church regularly and worship with others and yet, to all intents and purposes, completely disregard others in the body or disregard their own calling to serve that body. In fact, the body picture shows us how much we need each other and how much we need to admit our vulnerability and inadequacy in reflecting Christ on our own. How grateful we should be for our brothers and sisters in the church, and how we should strive for unity. How much we should pray for ourselves and the church that we will go on growing in the gospel, in love, in Christ, and in the power of the Spirit, that we may eventually attain **to the whole measure of the fullness of Christ** (v. 13).

2

Walk no longer as the Gentiles walk
(Ephesians 4:17-32)

The apostle now develops further how the church should live and behave (walk) under the Lordship of Christ. In fact, this now makes up the majority of the rest of the letter. First, he develops a negative picture of the world in which the Ephesian Christians live and of the world's thought forms and behaviour (vv. 17-19). Then, by way of contrast, he describes the Christian life and way of thinking (vv. 20-24), before moving on to some very specific injunctions and applications of this (vv. 25-32).

> So I tell you this, and insist on it in the Lord, that you must no longer live as the Gentiles do, in the futility of their thinking. They are darkened in their understanding and separated from the life of God because of the ignorance that is in them due to the hardening of their hearts. Having lost all sensitivity, they have given themselves over to sensuality so as to indulge in every kind of impurity, with a continual lust for more (4:17-19).

The Ephesian Christians were largely converted from a Gentile background (see 3:1), as we have seen. Paul is now adamant as he says **I tell you this, and insist on it in the Lord**. He insists that their lives and thought forms must not any longer reflect the values of the **Gentiles**.

a) Pagans: the futility of thinking (4:17-18)

In 2:1-2 Paul had reminded them that, before coming to faith, they had lived in darkness following the ways of the world. There he had gone on to speak of the amazing love of the Lord in showing them mercy and providing for their salvation through his grace. But here Paul is concerned that their behaviour truly reflect this change of life that has happened as they have turned to Christ and now find themselves *in Christ*. There is a **futility** of **thinking** in the life of those who do not follow Christ. Paul refers to it as **ignorance** and being **darkened in their understanding**. In modern English the word 'mindset' is sometimes used for what Paul talks of here. The non-Christian mind is set on a different path from the Christian mind. Paul clearly painted the picture of the goal of the Christian and of the church: it is to reflect Christ fully. This requires, as Paul says below in verse 23, being *made new in the attitude of your minds*. The mind controls our thinking and behaviour and the direction we wish to follow. If the mind of the Christian follows after the light, Jesus Christ, then the contrast with darkness is obvious. Paul develops this contrast in 5:8-14 as he speaks of the fruit of the light and living as 'children of light'.

Mention of **ignorance** has an Old Testament background and refers to a person's whole attitude to God, not just whether he understands something about God. Paul develops this argument in more detail in Romans 1:20-22. There he shows that something of God can be known even from his general revelation in creation and yet still people think they know better than God and have ignored what they see. Even if they have not been taught of the love and light in Jesus Christ, nevertheless they have still ignored and deliberately obscured even the revelation of God's power and divinity to be seen clearly all around them. Thus, this sort of 'ignorance' and 'futility of thinking' is held culpable before God (Rom. 1:32). Something of this is seen as Paul addresses the philosophers on the Areopagus in Acts 17. Even though they have an altar to 'an unknown god', their ignorance of the true God requires their repentance (Acts 17:30-31). Here in Ephesians Paul describes, as he did in Romans 1, a picture of the **hardening of** hearts. As people live **separated from the life of God**, so God is indeed separate from them and they become more and more hardened against him. They lose **all sensitivity** in the sense of not even being aware of their disobedience to God. It is like the person who has become so used to uttering blasphemy and coarse language at work that they are no longer even aware of when they are using such language. Darkness is so much part and parcel now of *who* they are, that it has affected every area of life, not just their lack of awareness of God, but also their own self-awareness and sensibilities.

b) Pagans: the impurity of life (4:19)

Following Paul's teaching in Romans 1:24 (God has given them over in the sinful desires of their heart ...), so their darkness becomes even darker and they **indulge in every kind of impurity, with a continual lust for more**. The word *impurity* probably refers to many different sexual sins. As those who get caught up in addiction to pornography or drugs discover, it only satisfies briefly, and always more is needed and expected of the next experience. Continually there is a **lust for more**.

Paul succeeds in his intention graphically to paint a disturbing picture of the life of those outside Christ. In 2:2 he had pointed out that this was the life many of them had been caught up in before the wonderful intervening grace of God in Christ which led to their salvation and transformation. His concern now is that their lives reflect the new reality, and so he turns to the positive description.

> You, however, did not come to know Christ that way. Surely you heard of him and were taught in him in accordance with the truth that is in Jesus. You were taught, with regard to your former way of life, to put off your old self, which is being corrupted by its deceitful desires; to be made new in the attitude of your minds; and to put on the new self, created to be like God in true righteousness and holiness. Therefore each of you must put off falsehood and speak truthfully to his neighbour, for we are all members of one body (4:20-25).

They have come to **know** Christ. The Greek is rather more remarkable here. Literally we read: 'Now you did not *learn* Christ that way.' This is a unique expression and Paul seems to have in mind two things as he uses it. There is the personal sense in which people came to know Christ as Saviour and Lord when they came to faith. There is also the body of Christ's teaching (and biblical teaching as a whole which all points to Christ) that they were given on becoming Christians and which they have been taught ever since by the apostles, evangelists, pastors and teachers. Right from the start, the Ephesian Christians have been taught that becoming a Christian is not simply hearing **of him** but also following **the truth that is in Jesus**.

The fact that Paul here uses the name **Jesus** (the only occasion in Ephesians where he does not link it with Lord or with Christ) may help us see his intention. The **truth** has not just been learned and taught but has been seen in the person of Jesus. If Christians wish to know what truth as a way of life looks like, they have been shown it **in Jesus**.

c) Christians: made new in their minds (4:20-23)

Paul continues to describe that this change in life, which they had been taught, should go along with commitment to Christ as Lord, and he does so with three verbs: **put off**, **be made new**, and **put on**. In fact, the distinction between the former way of life and the Christian way of life is so utterly remarkable that Paul talks of it as a *creation*. The **old self** designates the person whom Paul has described as set against God and living in darkness. It refers to the whole person, his actions, thoughts and behaviour. On becoming a Christian, this has been laid aside like an overcoat, and Paul wants to ensure that this remains the case for Christians in their day-to-day life. They must not revert to former ways (*you must no longer live ...* v. 17). But if one overcoat has been put off, another has been **put on**. And this enables Paul to make the contrast yet again. If the one is **corrupted** and **deceitful**, the other is a **new self**, one who in his whole person – his actions, thoughts and behaviour – is righteous and holy, Christ-like. If the whole person is to be changed in this way then being

made new in the attitude of [their] minds will be essential.[1] One mind will seek after the things of darkness, the other will seek and find the light in following Christ.

This extraordinary transformation in the person who has experienced God's grace has been described in earlier chapters, especially 2:4-5. There we read that *God, who is rich in mercy, made us alive with Christ*. In 2:10 Paul had written, *we are ... created in Christ Jesus to do good works*. In 2:15 he had described Christ's purpose as being *to create in himself one new man out of the two*. Whether Paul uses the analogy of resurrected life or talks of being **created to be like God**, the reader is constantly reminded that this transformation is by God and wholly of his grace. (He is the one who creates.) The picture of *creation*, however, is especially significant. In the creation of the world and of Adam and Eve God is seen to create 'out of nothing'. In a very real sense that same idea is carried forward in regeneration as people come to faith. It is entirely a work of God. As Paul says in 2 Corinthians 5:17: 'Therefore, if anyone is in Christ, he is a new creation; the old has gone, the new has come!'

d) Christians: to be like God (4:24-29)

Thus the depth of the transformation is clear for all to see as Paul spells it out: **created to be like God in true righteousness and holiness.** Paul could also have said 'like Christ'. 'In Christ' Christians are God's people. They are to reflect him, to 'image' him, as was intended in the original creation of Adam and Eve in the Garden of Eden. Righteousness and holiness describe a way of living life that demonstrates service, honour and obedience to God.

'**True** righteousness' may perhaps better be understood as 'coming from the truth'. In other words, these characteristics which Christians are to reflect, and which are attributes of God himself, come from the truth, from God and from Christ. Truly, the **new self** is to reflect God in all his truth. Is it any wonder

---

1 There is no distinction here between 'mind' and 'heart' in 1:18. The heart/mind is 'enlightened' by the Holy Spirit as part of the transforming work of God in the life of the believer.

that Paul should be concerned that those who are thus **new**, thus **created,** should walk the life worthy of this extraordinary calling? In verses 25-32 the apostle now expands the 'putting off' by way of various examples.

i) Putting off falsehood

The first concerns the contrast between truth and falsehood. **Therefore**, he says, truth will be a characteristic of this new life. **Falsehood** will be **put off** and replaced with speaking **truthfully** to a **neighbour**. With the use of the word 'neighbour' Paul reminds his readers of the great command of Leviticus 19:18: '*Do not seek revenge or bear a grudge against one of your people, but love your neighbour as yourself. I am the* LORD.'

Although these are instructions to which all individual Christians must pay attention in their own lives, Paul does not lose sight of the fact that each individual makes up the body, and it is the **one body** of which **we are all members**[2] which will prosper when its members speak truthfully to each other. It is a good reminder to all Christians that there is no place in God's church for deceit or dissimulation, no place for tendentious gossip, or for concealing the truth from each other.

ii) No more anger

'In your anger do not sin': Do not let the sun go down while you are still angry, and do not give the devil a foothold (4:26-27).

Paul now moves to a second practical command which helps to express clearly the type of transformation from old to new that should be seen in the life of one who is a new creation in Christ. Highlighting the three issues of **anger, stealing** and **unwholesome talk**, Paul touches on sins common to most people. Each command, however, is linked to a positive result, so helping the reader understand that God's commands are not simply arbitrary but have useful practical outcomes as well as reflecting his own image.

---

2 Greek: 'members of one another.'

In your anger do not sin is a quotation from Psalm 4:4. In that psalm, David is being attacked by his enemies unfairly. He knows this attack emanates from those who are not only set against him but also against God. He turns to the Lord for help and finds great joy (4:7), and that he can indeed *sleep in peace* because the Lord lets him dwell in safety (4:8). So Paul encourages others not to let this anger degenerate into sin as they get (righteously and understandably) angry in the light of unfair attacks upon them.

They should ensure that, at least by the end of the day, they have turned to the Lord for the comfort and peace and joy that they so need. For most of us it is all too easy to let that righteous anger (the deep frustration and hurt and desire to see justice done in the face of unjust accusation) descend into sin, as we begin to think evil thoughts against others and perhaps even look at ways of acting against them. Thus Paul, following the psalmist's own experience, says that it is right to deal with the anger and leave vengeance in the hands of the Lord, thus not giving **the devil a foothold**. In 6:11 Paul begins a section encouraging believers to stand against the Devil. Not letting the sun go down on our anger provides an excellent example of the sort of practical way in which we *stand our ground* against the Devil day by day. The same may be said of the following, third command which addresses the case of stealing.

iii) No more stealing

> He who has been stealing must steal no longer, but must work, doing something useful with his own hands, that he may have something to share with those in need (4:28).

Here Paul assumes that some of these converts have been stealing, probably in their past unconverted lives, but perhaps this behaviour has not yet been fully dealt with and so he says **no longer**. The alternative is to **work, doing something useful** (good) **with his own hands**. This not only enables the individual to escape sin, but, as Paul is always keen to show, it benefits the body because in his work he will gain enough for himself and **have something to share with those in need**. Doing something 'good' points us back to the conclusion of Paul's wonderful passage on the grace that Christians experience 'in Christ'. There we read in 2:10 that *we are God's workmanship, created in Christ Jesus to do good works, which God prepared in advance for us to do*. Given the mention of creation here in 4:24 (as in 2:10), Paul wants us to see the contrast proposed here is between doing that which is of the Devil and doing that which has been prepared for us to do by God.

iv) No unwholesome talk

> Do not let any unwholesome talk come out of your mouths,
> but only what is helpful for building others up according
> to their needs, that it may benefit those who listen (4:29).

The fourth example and command concerns bad language. We are all too aware of the nature of **unwholesome talk**. This talk may be what we would call 'foul language' or even blasphemy, but it may be much less obvious than that. Such talk may include gossip or simply always criticising others or criticising the church. How quickly is a local church divided when people's unwholesome talk begins to chip away at unity with the nasty undercurrent it creates. Such people have indeed given a foothold for the Devil.

That Paul has in mind conversation in and around the church and the damage that can be done seems to be supported by the positive side of this command. The opposite is conversation that **is helpful for building others up according to their needs**. How often have those of us who are church leaders almost despaired as we have seen the damage done to whole congregations by one or two people who constantly find fault or always seem to be tearing down rather than **building others up**. Yet, conversely, how wonderful are the men and women in any congregation who have learned this lesson and who set about bringing some conversation to people that **may benefit** (give grace to) **those who listen**. Such encouragers, such godly, righteous and holy people, are the backbone of a united church. We need to pray that we ourselves may learn from them and that our churches will see the *grace* of this gift develop deeply throughout the church.

e) Christians: not to grieve the Spirit (4:30)

And do not grieve the Holy Spirit of God, with whom you were sealed for the day of redemption (4:30).

For the sealing of **the Holy Spirit** see the more lengthy comments on 1:13-14. We noted there that what the Holy Spirit guarantees is that, at the future day when Christ will return to judge, God's people will be *seen* to be redeemed. Christ's return can be called 'the day of the Lord', 'the day of wrath', the day of 'judgment', and so on, but the wonderful description used by Paul here refers to it as **the day of redemption**. The destiny of those who believe is certain. They will be redeemed and the Holy Spirit guarantees it. There need be no fear of Christ's return or of the judgment day for those who are 'in Christ'. How much more then should those **sealed** people strive not to **grieve the Holy Spirit of God**. Grieving means that hurt and pain may be caused to the Holy Spirit of God. This becomes a very powerful and persuasive argument for Christians to behave in a way which truly reflects the God by whom they are redeemed.

Given the reference to redemption as well as the grieving of the Spirit, it is likely that Paul has Isaiah 63:9-10 in mind as he writes. There the prophet recalled the way the people of God, the Israelites, had grieved the Holy Spirit: 'In his love and mercy he redeemed them; he lifted them up and carried them all the days of old. Yet they rebelled and grieved his Holy Spirit.' However, one of the great privileges and joys of the new covenant and being 'in Christ' is that even sins that might grieve the Holy Spirit are forgiven 'in Christ', and so Paul says that they **were sealed** (past tense). How different this is from what then happened to the Israelites as recounted in Isaiah 63:10: 'So he (God) turned and became their enemy and he himself fought against them.'

There is a special link between the Holy Spirit and *speaking* in Scripture. It is for this reason, perhaps, that Paul links the grieving of the Holy Spirit with *unwholesome talk*. In 5:18-19 we see that being filled with the Spirit will lead to speaking *to one another with psalms, hymns and spiritual songs*. Thus, unwholesome talk is a very special example of turning against the Spirit or ignoring his influence in the Christian's life. Rather the Spirit's direct influence will be seen when a person's words build up other people **according to their needs**, and when the body of Christ is benefited by what is spoken.

f) Christians: people who forgive (4:31-32)

Another example and command is now given which also carries with it a positive alternative to the behaviour which is condemned.

> Get rid of all bitterness, rage and anger, brawling and slander, along with every form of malice. Be kind and compassionate to one another, forgiving each other, just as in Christ God forgave you (4:31-32)

All the words Paul uses here seem to expand upon the notion of anger which he has spoken about in verse 26. The words all contribute to a feeling of lack of self-control. The tragedy of burning anger and bitterness in a person's life is something that is sadly seen all too often in the society around us. Often it goes hand in hand with people being nasty to or even fighting with each other. Certainly underneath it all often lies a very deep inability to forgive a past wrong that may have been done to the person. The alternative expected of those who are the Lord's people is that they should be **kind and compassionate to one another**. Once again Paul is thinking of how Christians treat other Christians within the body. Forgiveness will be a mark of this **new self** because it will be modelled on God and on Christ, and **in Christ God forgave** the believer.

It is important to remember that both the negative (get rid of) and the positive (be kind) aspect of this command take real effort. Kindness and compassion are not the natural possession of fallen and, therefore, unspiritual men and women. But they are possible in the power of the Holy Spirit as believing men and women look to God to defeat sin and to enable them to live lives that *do not give the devil a foothold*. Paul will write in chapter 6 about the armour, given by God, that will protect and enable God's people to behave according to the new self rather than the old.

Summary of Chapter 4

God's people have an extraordinary inheritance in Christ. As his people, then, they should reflect God's blessing and his light to the world not only in what they say, but also in how they live. This chapter has exhorted us to be true to our calling. Unity in the church and patience, humility and love among ourselves will be essential. Paul has taken time to explain that this unity is based in God himself. There is one Lord and one faith, as there is one God and Father, and therefore we reflect this in being *one* body. But such unity is only possible through God's grace. This grace is seen in the way God gives gifts to his people so that each person may be an active part of the body in which all are being built up in faith and unity. The goal of this united body is that we may reach such maturity together in Christ that we reflect the *One Lord*, the *fullness of Christ*.

This maturity will help God's people better fend off the temptation to sin and better to present themselves as a holy people. Paul then describes the futility of pagan thinking and life and urges God's people to be renewed in their minds, and reflect God himself in righteousness and holiness.

3

Walk in love
(Ephesians 5:1-7)

Time and again through chapter 4 we have seen that the goal of the Christian life and of God's people as the body of Christ is to reflect God and Christ. Now Paul pulls this underlying thought to the front as, for the third time, he talks of how Christians should 'walk'.

The first two verses of chapter 5 both look backwards to chapter 4 and forward to the first section of chapter 5 (vv. 1-7) in Paul's discussion. Again Paul presents the positive and negative sides of the life that is to be lived. This time he begins with the positive command to **live a life of love** and showing how Christ's death provides a model for this. He then moves on to show the evil of living a life that is centred in self-indulgence, immorality and greed.

a) A life of self-sacrifice in imitation of God (5:1-2)

> Be imitators of God, therefore, as dearly loved children and live a life of love, just as Christ loved us and gave himself up for us as a fragrant offering and sacrifice to God (5:1-2).

We saw in 1:5 that Christians have been *adopted as his [God's] sons through Jesus Christ* and it is this covenant family picture that Paul has in mind here. We use the expression 'Like father like son', and so it should be of Christians. We are to imitate God in all we do. Elsewhere on several occasions Paul has talked of God as 'Father' (1:17; 2:18; 3:14) but here he simply talks of us as his **children.** We have seen how the Christian is to be 'like God' in righteousness and holiness (4:24). But we have also seen that, if we want to know what God is like, we must look to Jesus. This was clear in the last verse (4:32) where we believers were called upon to be forgiving 'because *in Christ* God forgave you'. Just as we have seen the significance and joy of what it is to be 'in Christ' as we studied the first two chapters of this epistle, so now we see the ethical implications of the same little phrase. As we look at Christ in action, we see God in action. As God forgave, he did so in Christ. Here in 5:1 we are **dearly loved children** and in verse 2 we discover that God's love for us is shown in how **Christ loved us**.

The description of Christ's love for us is expanded to remind the reader of his voluntary sacrificial death on behalf of his people. In one way, it is of course impossible for anyone to follow in the footsteps of Christ's sacrifice. Even if a Christian should give his life for another person, it will not achieve the redemption and forgiveness achieved by Christ on the cross. This aspect of Christ's death is drawn out by the emphasis on the fact that Christ **gave himself up for us**. This voluntary giving of himself on the cross was for all members of his body, **for us**, that is for those who believe. The words indicate both Christ's representative death on behalf of his people[1] and his substitutionary sacrifice on their behalf. As substitute, Christ's sacrificial death stands in the place of the death that would otherwise have been required for sin.

It is particularly this substitutionary aspect of Christ's self-giving sacrifice on the cross that Paul has in mind here. Though its redemptive work is something never to be repeated by anyone, nevertheless, it provides the supreme picture of what true love really looks like. And so Paul calls people to look at Christ and see the total commitment to each other that is required if we are to love like God loves. Paul will give another example of this sort of Christ-like loving commitment when he talk to husbands and wives in 5:25-28.

The challenge of these few short words is extraordinary. Love is not some nice gentle 'feeling', or something that

---

1 In his death Christ represents his people so that Paul can say *one has died for all: therefore all have died* (2 Cor. 5:14).

simply sounds good when we talk about it, but it is costly and involves real personal sacrifice. As members of the body of Christ, as God's **dearly loved children**, this is how Christian men and women are to behave with each other. It is this sort of love that puts the other first which will build up the body of Christ, the love that is prepared to put aside one's own comforts and well-being for the sake of the other and that always seeks the best for those around. It is this sort of love that will demonstrate the worship and thanksgiving that is due to the Lord who so willingly gave himself for his people.

b) Contrast: a life of self-indulgence and idolatry leading to judgment (5:3-7)

The apostle now moves to show the opposite of imitating God and his love seen in Christ. This opposite is to be found in self-indulgent greed.

> But among you there must not be even a hint of sexual immorality, or of any kind of impurity, or of greed, because these are improper for God's holy people. Nor should there be obscenity, foolish talk or coarse joking, which are out of place, but rather thanksgiving. For of this you can be sure: No immoral, impure or greedy person – such a man is an idolater – has any inheritance in the kingdom of Christ and of God. Let no one deceive you with empty words, for because of such things God's wrath comes on those who are disobedient. Therefore do not be partners with them (5:3-7).

In Scripture **sexual immorality** (a very broad term applied to a variety of different sexual sins) and **impurity** are often linked with **greed** (v. 5). Indulgence in immoral activity has to do with self-gratification, usually without much thought for anyone else involved or without concern for the impact of such behaviour on other people. These activities (already mentioned in 4:19) are **improper for God's holy people**. As we have seen already, they stand against all that it is to be a **holy** people. God's people will put his will first and will seek to build others up and love others with a self-sacrificial

attitude towards them. This point is made in a dramatic way
in verse 5. In common with a number of places in Scripture,
immorality and greed are linked with idolatry. Putting one's
own desires and lusts first rather than putting God and his
way and his people first, means God's position is usurped
– **such a man is an idolater.**

The Ephesian Christians were *idolaters* before turning to
Christ. Paul has rejoiced greatly in the opening two chapters
at the wonderful inheritance that belongs to those who are
holy and *in Christ.* He has shown that they are new creations
and made alive in Christ. To behave immorally as an idolater
is dangerous indeed. That life marked out the old man and
should be fully in the past but, if it isn't, then the reader
should remember that such a person has no **inheritance in
the kingdom of Christ and of God**. We are reminded of the
change of lordships we talked about in 1:7. There is a way of
walking, of life and behaviour that is to be distinctive of **the
kingdom of Christ and of God,** and a way that will be typical
of those who follow *the ruler of the kingdom of the air* (2:2).

The concern here is that someone may **deceive with empty
words** and cause those in the church at Ephesus to become
disobedient. This is precisely the way of life they *used to walk*
(2:2) but from which they had been redeemed. They had been
by nature objects of wrath (2:3), but through God's great mercy
are now *made alive*. Becoming **partners with** such followers of
evil leads to the **wrath** of God.

In this day and age the warning has lost none of its force.
In our churches in the west there are teachers and leaders
who deceive God's people by seeking to argue that various
forms of sexual immorality prohibited in Scripture are simply
'culturally conditioned' and need not apply to Christians
today. Combine that false teaching with the temptation and
pressure in western societies towards so-called sexual freedom
and personal choice and the warning of Paul in these verses
must not be allowed to fall on deaf ears or to be overlooked.
There was and remains a behaviour that is so **improper for
God's people,** and so much the opposite of the light that God
has revealed for the way we should live as his **holy** people,
that it should not even get a voicing among us – **not even**

a hint. Even the words and sentences coming from the mouth of a believer should reflect their holiness of life. **Coarse joking and obscenity** are ways of speaking about immorality or joking about wrong behaviour or wrong attitudes to sexual immorality. But even here, Paul reminds the reader of what should take its place, and it comes back again to building up the community and focusing on God in Christ: there should be **thanksgiving**. Chapters 1 and 2 have specially spelled out all the reasons for thanksgiving that we have in Christ.

The idea of kingdoms and lordships continues as Paul now develops the contrast between light and darkness, and talks in verse 8 of being *children of light*. In Colossians 1:12 this concept of kingdoms and the joy of thanksgiving that has been discussed is drawn together succinctly: 'joyfully giving thanks to the Father, who has qualified you to share in the inheritance of the saints in the kingdom of light. For he has rescued us from the dominion of darkness and brought us into the kingdom of the Son he loves.'

4

Walk as children of the Light
(Ephesians 5:8-14)

Recalling the contrast he made (2:2-3) between what the Ephesian Christians were and what they now are, Paul reiterates all that he has been saying:

> For you were once darkness, but now you are light in the Lord. Live as children of light (for the fruit of the light consists in all goodness, righteousness and truth) and find out what pleases the Lord. Have nothing to do with the fruitless deeds of darkness, but rather expose them. For it is shameful even to mention what the disobedient do in secret. But everything exposed by the light becomes visible, for it is light that makes everything visible. This is why it is said: 'Wake up, O sleeper, rise from the dead, and Christ will shine on you' (5:8-14).

Darkness is the realm of evil and that which is set against the Lord and his people. In chapter 6 we shall see that there is an ongoing battle that must be fought against the spiritual forces which lie behind such darkness. 'For our struggle is ... against the powers of this dark world' (6:12). But here the Ephesians are reminded not that they were once living in the realm of darkness, but that they **were once darkness**. Darkness and its dominion is itself mediated through people who sin and do not follow the Lord. They represent the kingdom they serve and hence **were** themselves darkness. The joy for the Christian, though, is that the same holds true with the light. It is not just that believers live in the realm of Light, which they do, but they are identified with the Lord himself.[1] They are **in the Lord** and so they **are light.** And so for the fourth time Christians are reminded to take note of how they should *walk* and behave: **Live** (walk) **as children of light**. There is a direct contrast here with those who are *sons of disobedience* in verse 6 and in 2:2 (NIV – *who are disobedient*).

Christians are related as family, **children**, to the one who is Light, to God and to Christ. God and light are often linked in the Old Testament as in Psalm 89:15 where God's people are therefore expected to live accordingly: 'Blessed are those who have learned to acclaim you, who walk in the light of your presence, O LORD.' Of course, in the New Testament Jesus speaks of himself as the Light and expects those who follow him to reflect that light: 'I am the light of the world. Whoever follows me will never walk in darkness, but will have the light of life' (John 8:12).

Being **light** provides a motivation for being Christ-like and so the **fruit** is spelled out in similar terms to those used in 4:24. The Lord is good, righteous, and true, and it must be the same for those who are **in the Lord**. It thus becomes self-evident why those in the Lord can have **nothing to do with the fruitless deeds of darkness**, nor even talk of the things that **the disobedient do in secret** (vv. 11-12).

As we have seen before, though, there is specific action that will be needed by believers as they seek to walk in the Light and follow the Lord. They will need to **find out what pleases the Lord**. In other words, they will need constantly to be aware of that which is good, righteous and of the truth and follow those things, thus doing the Lord's will. They need constantly to be aware of that which may deceive them and draw them into darkness. Christians will need to pray, to read Scripture, and work together as a body to follow Christ.

---

1 Perhaps Paul recalled the words of Isaiah 9:2: 'The people walking in darkness have seen a great light; on those living in the land of the shadow of death a light has dawned.'

But it is above all the Holy Spirit who will work in the body and the life of the individual to draw attention to what is right and pleasing to the Lord. That is why Paul has *kept* praying that they may be given *the Spirit of wisdom and revelation, so that [they] may know him better* (1:17; see also 3:16; 5:18).

However, there is something else that happens when light comes into contact with darkness and that is that things of the dark are exposed. Even when a small match or candle is lit in a large dark room, it is surprising how much is revealed by the light. And this is the point Paul now makes.

> Have nothing to do with the fruitless deeds of darkness, but rather expose them. ...everything exposed by the light becomes visible, for it is light that makes everything visible.[2]

Although the thought here is not entirely clear, the idea is that light makes even that which is dark become light. As Christians point out the activities of darkness by shining the light of Christ upon them, so those activities, often done **in secret**, are seen for what they are, immoral and impure (verse 5), fruitless (v. 11), and shameful (v. 12). As this light is shone upon the darkness, so there is the anticipation that those in darkness may themselves turn to light, and so what is revealed becomes **light** (v. 14). In other words, Paul anticipates that the witness of *the children of light*, as they expose sin for what it is, will lead the *sons of disobedience* to seek this light of the Lord and to find his love and grace. After all, this is exactly what had happened to the Ephesian Christians themselves (2:1-5).

This section is then summed up with what appears at first glance to be a biblical quotation:

> This is why it is said: 'Wake up, O sleeper, rise from the dead, and Christ will shine on you.'

It may well have been a Christian hymn based on Isaiah 60:1. If so, then the prophet helps us see what Paul means; the prophet

---

2 Greek: 'for all that is revealed is light.'

says: 'Arise, shine, for your light has come, and the glory of the LORD rises upon you.' The very next verses in Isaiah 60 speak of *darkness* being over the earth and the people. But the prophet sees hope: 'but the LORD rises upon you and his glory appears over you. Nations will come to your light, and kings to the brightness of your dawn' (Isa. 60:2-3). Isaiah looks forward to the time which Paul has seen among the Ephesian Christians as they have turned from darkness to light with the coming of the Lord (Jesus).

But Paul anticipates this continuing to happen. As light exposes darkness, so more will turn to 'the brightness of your [Israel: God's people's] dawn'. Thus, with support from Scripture, Paul provides yet another wonderful motivation to *find out what pleases the Lord* and to *live as children of light.*

Further Application

It is worth pausing here to take stock of these opening verses of chapter 5.

First, we need to understand the nature of Christian love. 'Love', in the modern usage of the word, is little more than an emotion or feeling. It switches on and off in our relationships depending on how we feel about a person that day. Many would feel that obedience and love are actually opposed to each other. Love cannot be compelled; it is a feeling that is either present or not present. Yet for Christians, the supreme example of love that we are called to follow is to be found in Christ's obedience, even to the point of giving his life. Christ's love for us is seen, says Paul, in his sacrifice on the cross. Christian love is a love that God *commands*. It has to be worked at and sometimes that work is hard and even discouraging. But as children of God we are to go where he wants and that will involve working at loving those who are often 'unlovable' – people like you and me.

*Secondly, we must understand that appearances **do** matter.* Living as 'children of Light' means being *seen*. This passage asks us continually to be vigilant about how others may see us. All too often there is a disjunction between what we affirm in church on Sundays and how we appear at work or in the family. Paul doesn't beat around the bush when he says things like 'no coarse joking'. We can think of the laughter in the office, or the comedy shows on TV, and realise that all too often there is a 'hint of impurity'. We may be quick to condemn sexual immorality and yet flirt at work. Then there is greed! I am increasingly convinced that, in the Western world, this is where we all flounder and fail to be the Light we should be. The big house, the attention to dress, to style, to cars, all (at the very least) often give a 'hint of our greed'. How far these things are from the 'fruit of the Light' which 'consists in all goodness, righteousness and truth'!

5

Walk wisely
(Ephesians 5:15–6:9)

For the fifth time in these last two chapters Paul urges Christians to watch how they **live**. Having contrasted the realms of light and darkness, Paul now takes up another contrast well known from the Old Testament, the contrast between wisdom and foolishness. He begins with some general application of this to the family of the church before using three examples of relationships within the Christian household. This section therefore runs right through to 6:9.

a) Wise or foolish (5:15-17)

> Be very careful, then, how you live – not as unwise but as wise, making the most of every opportunity, because the days are evil. Therefore do not be foolish, but understand what the Lord's will is (5:15-17).

The sort of wisdom to which Paul is referring here has to do not just with a knowledge of God and of Jesus but an ability to live as God wants. Foolishness is the exact opposite of this. The word is used to refer to the way of (practical) living among those who have ignored God's law or who are not his people. The 'wisdom literature' of the Old Testament makes this very clear. For example, in Proverbs 16:23 we read: 'A wise man's heart guides his mouth, and his lips promote instruction.' Or again, in Proverbs 21:20: 'In the house of the wise are stores of choice food and oil, but a foolish man devours all he has.' This sort of wisdom is one that seeks to follow the law of the Lord in day to day life. It has a very practical outworking. Jesus himself built on this understanding of wisdom and folly in the parable of the ten virgins in Matthew 25.

So Paul's appeal here becomes even more practical. There is a need to **understand what the Lord's will is** not merely for the sake of having more knowledge but for the sake of life itself. Paul will go on to show the role the Holy Spirit has in this necessity (v. 18), but here he makes it clear that the opposite of being **foolish** is understanding the will of the Lord. (More was said of this in looking at 5:10.)

making the most of every opportunity might better be translated as *making the most of the time*. It is thus an appeal to Christians to live a godly, righteous and truthful life day by day, and not to waste any of the time in ignoring the will of the Lord or being disobedient. The fact that **the days are evil** reminds us that all Christian living awaits the final day when Christ returns but, as we have seen in the preceding verses, living now in the light, in accordance with the will of the Lord, will enable the light to shine in the darkness and perhaps turn others to the Lord.

As Christians, we must never discount the effect of righteous living, of living as **wise** people in a world of darkness. It is all too easy to assume that the way we live will not have any impact on anyone, and yet it will help other believers understand the **Lord's will,** and it will reveal wisdom to those who, at present, only know foolishness and **evil**.

Paul now uses a practical example of foolishness and contrasts that way of living with the way of wisdom.

b) Drunk or Spirit-filled (5:18)

Do not get drunk on wine, which leads to debauchery. Instead, be filled with the Spirit (5:18).

Drunkenness is a classic practical example of unwise living. Paul may specifically have in mind Proverbs 20:1: 'Wine is a mocker and beer a brawler; whoever is led astray by them is not wise.' Drunkenness achieves nothing for the individual except loss of self-control, and certainly does nothing to build up the body of Christ. It becomes, therefore, a representative example of all **foolish** behaviour which, by definition, achieves nothing for the individual and their relationship with the Lord nor for the body of Christ. Given that Paul has been talking of light and darkness, he may have in mind the idea that drunkenness is often seen at night. This is what he puts forward in similar teaching in 1 Thessalonians 5:5-8:

> You are all sons of the light and sons of the day. We do not belong to the night or to the darkness. So then, let us not be like others, who are asleep, but let us be alert and self-controlled. For those who sleep, sleep at night, and those who get drunk, get drunk at night. But since we belong to the day, let us be self-controlled, putting on faith...

But there is an alternative, **be filled with the Spirit**. Alcohol and the Spirit have an affect on the person. The fruit of the one is a loss of self-control (see Prov. 25:28; 2 Tim. 3:3), the fruit of the other is the finding of self-control (Gal. 5:23). Paul has already talked in relation to the church as the body of Christ of *the fullness of him who fills everything* (1:23). When looking at 3:19 we discussed the meaning of Paul's prayer for the Ephesians that they should be *filled to the measure of all the fullness of God*.

There we said, 'This is the goal of Christians. It can also be described as becoming Christ-like (see 4:13). Our goal as individuals and supremely as the church, the body of Christ, is fully to reflect the image of God.... As we come to know and experience the wonder of Christ's love at work deep within us, so we will go on and on being filled with the Spirit.'

Be filled with the Spirit is thus to be seen as a present command to those who possess the Spirit and who know him as the *deposit guaranteeing* their *inheritance* (1:14). It is by the Spirit that they will know and experience the power for the life they are expected to live, and it is he who will enable them to *find out what pleases the Lord* and to *understand what the Lord's will is* (5:10, 17). It is only by this constant in-filling of the Spirit that God's people will truly begin to reflect the image of God and of Jesus. Instead of alcoholic drink being allowed to take hold of a person and change his or her behaviour, the Spirit must be allowed to bring about the change necessary so that folly may be replaced by wisdom and the ways of darkness exchanged for the ways of light.

c) The results of being Spirit-filled (5:19-20)

The command which then follows is little more than Paul's summary of the result of the filling of the Spirit in the body of Christ.

> Speak to one another with psalms, hymns and spiritual songs. Sing and make music in your heart to the Lord, always giving thanks to God the Father for everything, in the name of our Lord Jesus Christ (5:19-20).

People who are being filled with the Spirit will give the thanks to God that Paul had called for in 5:4. Paul himself at the start of the letter had provided an example of this when he said, 'I have not stopped giving thanks for you, remembering you in my prayers' (1:16). Though, as we shall see, Paul has specially in mind the thanksgiving of worship together within the body, such thanksgiving is to be constant through life, **always**. It is to be given to **God the Father**. He is the creator of all and the source of all goodness. Especially he is the one who Christians know 'has blessed us in the heavenly realms with every spiritual blessing in Christ' (1:3). But we praise and give thanks **in the name of our Lord Jesus Christ**. The *name* summarises all that he is, and it is because of what he is and what he has done, for the believer in redemption and in gaining access to the Father, that thanksgiving can be and should be done in his name.

This thanksgiving is the content of the singing and speaking that Paul mentions here. The filling of the Spirit will result in two things happening that Paul has referred to on several occasions over the last couple of chapters. First, the body will be built up and, secondly, the Lord will be praised and thanked.

Speak to one another with psalms, hymns and spiritual songs has to do with the body, the church. The words of the hymns will be part of how the body is built up in the Lord. It is very unlikely that there is any distinction to be made between these three words used for the songs that are sung by the church at worship. Rather what is important is that these are **spiritual**, that is, reflecting God's truth. They are not inspired in some sort of unintelligible way, in fact far from it. The whole point here is that these psalms and hymns will communicate the clear message and teaching about God and about Jesus so that Christians build each other up in the Lord.

Here a very similar passage in Colossians 3:15-17 is particularly enlightening and may help us see how Paul regards even the singing as part of the way Christians teach and admonish each other:

> Let the peace of Christ rule in your hearts, since as members of one body you were called to peace. And be thankful. Let the word of Christ dwell in you richly as you teach and admonish one another with all wisdom, and as you sing psalms, hymns and spiritual songs with gratitude in your hearts to God. And whatever you do, whether in word or deed, do it all in the name of the Lord Jesus, giving thanks to God the Father through him.

The second thing that happens is that Christians sing **to the Lord**. Paul has spelled out at great length in the opening chapters the joy Christians have in Christ, and so, as they **sing and make music**, they do so *with* their **heart**. That is, their joy wells up from the depths of their being, to Christ, the Lord. Interestingly, the place from which praise and singing and music spring up is precisely the place where the Spirit and Christ himself dwell (3:16-17). There is no sense here, as might be implied by the NIV translation, of anything private or silent in this worship. It is the same speaking and singing of psalms and hymns and spiritual songs which both brings praise to the Lord and also provides edification for the believers.

Once again we see something of the profound value of corporate worship. Sometimes we tend to think these days of our personal and private worship even when we gather together for our church services. We sing hymns because they make us feel good or say things about God that we want to hear. So often our attitude to worship, though well intentioned, is ultimately selfish. We ignore the fact that Spirit-filled people show the presence of the Spirit in their worship as they use hymns and songs to speak to each other, telling of the truths of the faith in ways designed to build each other up in the Lord. We forget that our thanksgiving comes from all of us gathered singing to the Lord who has called us to be his people, his body.

There is considerable discussion among commentators as to whether verse 20 goes with what has gone before or with what follows. The position taken here, as we indicated earlier, is that the whole of this section holds together right through until 6:9.

> Submit to one another out of reverence for [in the fear of] Christ (5:20).

To begin with we see, then, how this verse adds to what Paul has been saying about what is **wise** and **unwise**. Wise people are those who are Spirit-filled (v. 18) and who are **careful** about how they *walk* (v. 15). A more literal translation will help demonstrate how Paul's thought is moving: the result of the command, *Be filled with the Spirit*, is that the body will be built up and thanksgiving offered to the Lord. This is achieved by (i) speaking to one another with psalms, (ii) singing and making music to the Lord, (iii) always giving thanks to God and, now, (iv) *submitting to one another*.

This submission is enjoined of all Christians and has to do with how they treat each other. The verse reminds us of what Paul has already said in this letter in 4:2: 'Be completely humble and gentle; be patient, bearing with one another in love.' The word **submit** normally has to do with ordering oneself under another person or under other people. For Christians it comes back to what Paul has been saying: they are constantly to build up the body of Christ. Rather than put themselves forward in the way that so often happens in modern society (and happened in Paul's day), they will put others first.

Above all, Christians will be marked by humility in their dealings with each other. Philippians 2:3 provides the most complete summary of what this submission will be like: 'Do nothing out of selfish ambition or vain conceit, but in humility consider others better than yourselves.' This is precisely what is meant by 'ordering oneself under others'. And in Philippians 2:5-8 Paul goes on to show that Christ himself provides the example on which Christians are to model themselves: 'Your attitude should be the same as that of Christ Jesus: Who, being in very nature God, did not consider equality with God something to be grasped, but made himself nothing, taking the very nature of a servant...'

Out of reverence for Christ is a fairly strong statement. The word 'reverence' carries the idea of *fear*. This is what Christ expects of his people because he is their Lord. Mutual submission is therefore not an optional extra when people are feeling good towards each other, or in agreement with each other, but it is a command that must be obeyed and worked at by all Christians at all times and in all relationships.

d) Spirit-filled household relationships – marriage (5:21-33)

i) Husbands and wives
It is very difficult for anyone to understand how, at the same time, it is possible to be submissive and yet also have particular role relationships with other people which may involve hierarchy. Yet this is precisely what we see in Jesus. Jesus is Lord of all. He is creator. He is the one Paul says is *in very nature God*, and yet he is also the one who, while having the role and status of Lord and redeemer and actually *being* God, can humble himself even to death for the sake of men and women. Paul will now go on in the last verses of Ephesians 5 to show what this sort of submission should look like in household relationships where different members of the household have particular roles. His point will be that roles, even where one has a position of leadership or authority over another, and submission are not at all mutually incompatible.

Paul considers three specific relationships within house-holds. What will submission look like in these most common of household relationships? For sure the relationships will look very different from what they looked like before the family's commitment to Christ.

The first example – the relationship between husband and wife – is developed at greatest length. Importantly Paul develops the theological basis for what he is saying and takes the reader back to the Lord Jesus Christ to see why things should be ordered as they are.

ii) Instructions for wives

> Wives, submit to your husbands as to the Lord. For the husband is the head of the wife as Christ is the head of the church, his body, of which he is the Saviour. Now as the church submits to Christ, so also wives should submit to their husbands in everything (5:21-24).

One of the reasons for suggesting that verse 20 both looks backwards to what has gone before (submission is a result of being filled with the Spirit) and looks forward to these specific relationships is that verse 21 has no verb. **Submit** here is drawn from the previous verse. Having given the general instruction, Paul now moves to a specific relationship in which **wives** are to **submit** to their **husbands**.

Few commands in Scripture create so many problems within much of the modern church. In a day when the equality of men and women is so strongly stressed, this verse seems to indicate the opposite. And yet that would be to ignore entirely what we have just spoken of in examining the question of mutual submission. The fact is that Christians today, in spite of the clear teaching of Scripture, do find it very hard to link mutual submission together with roles that may involve one person having some form of leadership or even authority over another. From the other side they also find it very hard indeed to exercise leadership in a context of mutual submission.

Before examining these verses it is worth looking at one other less controversial example where authority, leadership and submission come together. In 1 Peter 5:1-4 Peter speaks to elders. They are *overseers* of the church and yet they are called to exercise their leadership by serving and to be *willing* in their service. They are not to *lord it over* the flock but instead are to be an *example* to it, and again all this is because they follow the example of Christ himself. For Peter there is no sign of the apparently inherent contradiction between serving and having a role of authority and leadership.

This may help us now understand better the household relationship of wives and husbands. This verse, in line with other passages of Scripture, teaches a relationship of head-ship in which **the husband is the head of the wife**. In this relationship wives are to submit to their husbands **as to the Lord**. The motivation for the way they relate to their husband is that wives see this as part of their submission to the Lord. This submission will therefore be voluntary. It is not the husband's duty to enforce his wife's submission, but rather it is her role and joy to reflect the same submission to her husband as is seen when **the church submits to Christ**.

That Paul goes on to say **wives should submit to their husbands in everything** is an indication that he is thinking of their specific role within the family. This becomes clearer as Paul also explains to wives that **the husband is the head of the wife as Christ is the head of the church, his body, of which he is the Saviour**. In other words, husband and wife do not follow these roles because one is more intelligent or more dominant, or because one is more inclined to follow and another to lead. Rather they do so because God has called them **in the Lord** to pattern or image his relationship with his church, his people.

Christ is the **head of the church** specifically as its Lord. The church has been asked to *find out what the Lord's will is*. It is out of reverence or *fear* of Christ that all are called to submit themselves to each other. The wife is to reflect this relationship of the church to her Lord and Saviour as she relates to her husband. Marriage thus becomes the most extraordinary call-ing in which there is to be a picture of Christ's relationship with his church.

So often as the arguments over the roles of husbands and wives grow in intensity in the church in the twenty-first century, we forget that this model has always throughout the ages been a challenge to the cultural norms of the day, and so often it is completely forgotten that this is a *calling*. Paul is still talking to Christians about living lives *worthy of their calling* and about what it is to be Spirit-filled. Men and women, specifically called to live in a marriage relationship (i.e. not all men and all women at all times), are given the awesome duty of serving the Lord in this life-calling by modelling Christ in his love for the church (the husband) and the church in her submission and to her Lord (the wife). The fact that Paul refers again here to **the church,** as **his body** reminds us of the unity of this body and leads eventually into Paul's quotation of Genesis 2:24 in verse 31 – that husband and wife will be *united* and *the two become one flesh*. See below for a further discussion of marriage as a picture of God's love for his people and their response to a loving Lord.

iii) Instructions for husbands

Closely tied to what Paul says to wives is a longer section to husbands.

> Husbands, love your wives, just as Christ loved the church and gave himself up for her to make her holy, cleansing her by the washing with water through the word, and to present her to himself as a radiant church, without stain or wrinkle or any other blemish, but holy and blameless. In this same way, husbands ought to love their wives as their own bodies. He who loves his wife loves himself. After all, no one ever hated his own body, but he feeds and cares for it, just as Christ does the church – for we are members of his body (5:25-30).

As women are to submit to their husbands **as to the Lord,** so now husbands are told to **love** their wives **as Christ loved the church and gave himself up for her.** Husbands must still remember that verse 21 has applied to them. They are to submit to one another *out of reverence for Christ*. But this does not negate their God-given and creation-based calling to exercise a specific role within marriage when they are called to be husbands. If the wife plays out in life a wonderful witnessing picture of what it is to be the church in relationship to her Lord and Saviour, the husband is called to picture Christ in his self-giving love for the church who is seen as the bride.

In fact, Paul briefly expounds this picture of the church as the bride of Christ without using those words but by describing the church in bridal vocabulary. Thus she is **radiant, without stain or wrinkle or any other blemish and holy and blameless**. Interestingly, this was to the fore of Paul's thinking in 1:4 when he talked of the great blessings of God's people that were theirs *in Christ*. There we read that God 'chose us in him before the creation of the world to be *holy and blameless* in his sight'.

The church is seen as being presented by Christ as a pure virgin bride, a picture that is employed in a number of other places in Scripture. John the Baptist uses the imagery in John 3:29. In the book of Revelation the picture is developed more fully as the church is called 'a bride beautifully dressed for her husband' (21:2). The final day heralding the return of Christ is seen as a wedding in Revelation 19:7: 'Let us rejoice and be glad and give him glory! For the wedding of the Lamb has come, and his bride has made herself ready.'

Paul is building on the extraordinary commitment of Christ to his people as he exhorts husbands to live lives worthy of their calling and to demonstrate that they are filled with the Spirit. Christ **gave himself up** for the church so that she would find cleansing and forgiveness and salvation. Again the reference is to Christ's sacrifice for his people as in 5:2. In referring to Christ **cleansing her by the washing with water through the word**, attention is drawn to how the church is washed of her sin as she is forgiven and that this forgiveness comes to her by means of the **word** of God, the gospel of Christ, that has been preached to her.

What bigger counter-cultural challenge can there be across the ages for men who are so often filled with selfish desires and who put their own needs before anyone else's! Clearly acknowledging how hard this is for men, Paul points to their

ability almost automatically to look after their own needs:
**husbands ought to love their wives as their own bodies ...
no one ever hated his own body, but he feeds and cares for
it**. But Paul does not expect this to be sufficient motivation
for a man to love his wife and so he returns to say **just as
Christ does the church – for we are members of his body**.
The ultimate motivation for a husband to a rightly loving and
caring relationship with his wife is always Christ himself.

Here the husband is reminded that he is the *wife*!! He is part
of the church. He is a member of the body. He is loved by Christ
who gave himself for the Christian husband. He enjoys being
fed and cared for by Christ. He has received forgiveness and
he too is part of the body that is being presented **without stain**
and **holy and blameless**. If he truly sees how wonderful the
husband, Christ, is to him and his fellow believers, to the church,
then how much more will he seek to be the same sort of husband
to his wife. Such a husband will be loving and caring of his
wife. He will not force his will on his wife and he will treat her
with enormous love whatever position she takes towards him.
There is nothing here to say that he should be a good husband
only if she submits. There is nothing to say that if she doesn't
submit he should insist upon it or should be authoritarian in
the relationship. There is everything in this picture to say to
the husband that he should love as unconditionally and as self-
sacrificially as Christ loved his people.

And so Paul concludes by way of summary for both wife
and husband:

> 'For this reason a man will leave his father and mother and
> be united to his wife, and the two will become one flesh.'
> This is a profound mystery – but I am talking about Christ
> and the church. However, each one of you also must love
> his wife as he loves himself, and the wife must respect her
> husband (5:31-33).

When Paul thinks of marriage he thinks of a wife and a husband,
faithful and loyal and loving to each other, a submissive wife
and a husband who so loves his wife he is prepared to do
anything for her, even to the point of dying for her. But he

also thinks of something even more wonderful, a relationship that does not just last until we die, but a relationship that lasts through all eternity, the relationship of Christ to his people. Thus he says *this is a profound mystery – but I am talking about Christ and the church.*

As we saw in 3:3-9 the use of the word **mystery** has to do with how it is that 'in Christ' Jew and Gentile are brought together. It seems likely that the same thing is in mind here. Paul has just said in verse 30: **for we are members of his body**. In other words, Christ is the head of *his* one body (see 5:23). This is the astounding joy of being 'in Christ'. Here Jew and Gentile are brought together. Here the bride of Christ shines in her glory, and yet Paul is saying from Genesis 2 that, just as wife and husband, though two individuals, become one flesh, so it is with Christ and his church. This is surely *the measure of the fullness of Christ* in all his glory (4:13). Christ united with his church, united with both Jew and Gentile who are now found 'in Christ' and who are part of that holy and blameless people chosen in Christ *before the creation of the world* (1:4). This great marriage, arranged before the creation, comes to its climax at the wedding feast of the Lamb. For now, it offers the motivation for Christian husbands and Christian wives to show forth in their relationship the Lord's love for his church and his church's love for her Lord.

Further Application
As we have indicated above, there are few more delicate areas to tread around in the modern church than men and women's roles. However, a number of areas of application of Paul's teaching must be addressed.

First, the male headship referred to in this text is not authoritarian. In one sense this is obvious. If husbands model themselves on Christ then they will be humble servants rather than authoritarian masters.

However, the few models of headship available to Christian men in the world around them are almost universally authoritarian. Headship is only seen to be working when submission is seen. Thus, if submission is not seen, the 'head' or 'boss' will insist on it with threats of dismissal, lower pay, lack of promotion or whatever the situation requires. Instead of looking to Christ, the servant King, and asking how he exercises his authority in the church, husbands look to worldly models.

The 'macho' image of the tough 'he-man' is, sadly, all too common in some Christian circles. Men become bullies and, rather than letting their wives work out before God their own calling to submission, the husbands tell them how to behave. While this passage calls for both husbands and wives to fulfil their God-given roles, it does not tell husbands to insist on certain behaviour from their wives. Sadly, when men act in this way, often the gifts God has given their wives to use in the family, or in the world around, or in the church, remain entirely untapped. Instead of rejoicing in the gifts of their wives, men follow the world's models of authoritarian headship and often end up feeling threatened by their wives and start to put them down. Fulfilment of his role as a husband requires that a man constantly looks to Jesus and exercises a true, unconditional love and admiration for the one whom God, in his grace, has given him for a life-partner.

Secondly, wives are to submit as to the Lord. Again, this is obvious from the text but more difficult in practice. Women can also fail to follow the biblical picture in marriage. First, much as some men see their headship in the 'macho' image, some women see their submission in terms of weak passivity. Often working from a desire to serve the Lord properly in this area of life, they hide all their gifts, their intellectual abilities, and anything that might hint of taking an initiative in the home. The problem with this is that they have not examined how the church is called to be a Light to the world, to take the gospel initiative, to intercede for the world, to be compassionate and loving to all, and to wage a war against the 'principalities and powers' of this age. None of this speaks of weak passivity, but of a wife who will take initiative spiritually and in other ways in the family, who will ask her husband how he is before God, and who will intercede in prayer for him and the children. There is a unity of purpose between Christ and his church, and the wife should be actively striving for that as well as she consults, talks with, and urges her husband on so that together they live the picture of Christ and his church.

The picture that is constantly put in front of women in society today is one born of a feminist approach to life, and this leads to another set of problems for Christian women to face. Women act in the same sad strident way in which men act. They have to be omni-competent in the family, in the work place, in all that they do. They have to appear more 'macho' than the men with whom they now find they are in competition. Women who have grown up in this world find the whole concept of submission to be alien and old-fashioned. Again the need to look at Christ and his church is the only way through this. Love dressed in humility will focus on the person of Christ and ensure that the way life is lived is for the Lord's glory.

Thirdly, the lives lived by husbands and wives are not dependent on the response. This is true for both husbands and wives. Peter makes it very clear that a non-Christian husband may be won for Christ by seeing how his Christian wife lives (1 Pet. 3:1). Husbands are not told to love their wives only if they are 'lovable'! The picture of Christ that they are called to imitate is that he loved sinful and imperfect human beings. Men are to take this loving and caring role in the family however they may be treated.

Finally, what Paul says here does not apply to all men and all women. It is very important to note that Paul is talking about household relationships throughout this section of Ephesians. He is not saying that all women are to submit to all men whatever the circumstances, or that all men are to love all women as they love their own bodies. The love and submission described here is designed for husband and wife who have the very special calling of reflecting the relationship of Christ and his church.

Excursus: Marriage, a picture of God's love for his people

Paul shows that the theological basis for what he says about wives and husbands lies in the fact that marriage is designed by God in creation to be a picture of his relationship with his people. In other words, Paul does not work from marriage to Christ's love for the church but *from* Christ's love for the church to marriage. If marriage is understood in this way, then it becomes at least a little easier to see how vital *both* roles of husbands and wives are as they reflect the God/church relationship. The wife's submission and the particular words of 'love' and 'giving' used in relation to the husband are not intended to say wives cannot love or husbands cannot submit (Paul's whole previous argument has shown that cannot possibly be his intention). Rather they speak to the different roles in the acted drama that are given to husband and wife. The one is to be as Christ in this loving relationship and the other as the church.

As the husband loves his wife unselfishly even to the point of giving his life for her, he does so in a way that the whole world can witness and in which, God willing, the world will see something of Christ and his love for his people. As the wife in that same relationship willingly submits to her husband and seeks to follow his lead as her head, she does so in a way that the whole world can witness and in which, God willing, the world will see something of how the church is supposed to respond to such a loving Lord who was willing to die for his people.

This picture is not at all new, of course, to Ephesians or even to Paul's writing. From the very earliest of times God, though his prophets and in his law, has described his relationship with his people in terms of marriage. It is not the only picture the Bible uses to describe the relationship, but it is a very important one. Paul has spoken of the unity of the body and its union with Christ and 'in Christ', and he sees this as indicated right back in Genesis 2:24, which he now quotes in 5:31 as a final justification for what he has been saying: 'For this reason a man will leave his father and mother and be united to his wife, and the two will become one flesh.' Through the Old Testament, when God's people turn to other gods, rather than living united to him and under his husbandly loving rule, the Israelites are said to 'commit adultery'. God comes to his people in a way that should be recognisable to them because God gave them a picture right in creation itself: he comes as a loving husband. He woos his people with his love and they are to come to him in loving and willing submission because they fully trust him and his steadfast promises. In Deuteronomy 7:6-8 we read:

> The LORD your God has chosen you out of all the peoples on the face of the earth to be his people, his treasured possession. The LORD did not set his affection on you and choose you because you were more numerous than other peoples, for you were the fewest of all peoples. But it was because the LORD loved you ...

When Jeremiah speaks from God to his rebellious people he frequently talks of them as a wife who commits adultery. For example, in Jeremiah 3:6:

> During the reign of King Josiah, the LORD said to me, 'Have you seen what faithless Israel has done? She has gone up on every high hill and under every spreading tree and has committed adultery there.'

High on the hills were the altars to other gods. God wanted a faithful and submissive wife, but he also desired a people who would witness to his saving love for them. One of the most amazing portrayals of God's love for his people even as they turn away from him (committing adultery with idols) is to be found in the book of Hosea. There the prophet is asked to act out the role of God as a husband who so loves his unfaithful wife that he pursues her. It is an acted-out picture of God seeking after his people whom he has loved so much and yet who have not submitted to him and the loving lordship of his husbandly approaches. In Hosea 3:1 the Lord speaks to Hosea:

> The LORD said to me, 'Go, show your love to your wife again, though she is loved by another and is an adulteress. Love her as the LORD loves the Israelites, though they turn to other gods and love the sacred raisin cakes.'

With all this background combining with the injunction to marriage in Genesis 2, it becomes clear that already in creation

God had designed marriage to be a picture of himself in relationship with his people. What Paul does in Ephesians is to make thoroughly explicit how that prior relationship should now be acted out properly in the lives of believing couples. Thus, it is a glorious responsibility on the part of those called to be husbands and wives that, in walking a life worthy of their calling, they should reflect, as husbands, Christ and his love, and, as wives, the church and her submission to the loving Saviour.

It seems to this writer that it is only by coming to understand some of this background that we can begin to see why Paul says what he does. He is simply going right back to creation itself and saying 'this is why we have marriage': because we have a God who wants to be imaged in his loving, self-sacrificing relationship with his people and who wants a picture for all to see of the response he longs for from his people, a response of submission and trust.

e) Spirit-filled household relationships – children and parents (6:1-4)

The second relationship that is examined as Christians are helped to work out what it is to *walk wisely* and to be Spirit-filled in household relationships is that between parents and their children. This again is divided into two sets of instructions. The first is a command and encouragement for children and the second a warning for fathers.

i) Instructions for children

> Children, obey your parents in the Lord, for this is right. 'Honour your father and mother' – which is the first commandment with a promise – 'that it may go well with you and that you may enjoy long life on the earth' (6:1-3).

As with husbands and wives, the opening command here is a reminder that even children are answerable to the Lord for their behaviour. Finding out what the will of the Lord is for them, as they seek to live lives worthy of their calling and walk wisely, will also involve turning to Scripture. The apostle first commands that children **obey** their **parents**. They are under the authority of their parents but it is **in the Lord**. The children here are obviously at least of an age where they are young but responsible members of the church and are able to understand their relationship with their parents and with the Lord. Their obedience is the way that their particular submission will be shown within this household relationship.

Saying **for this is right** probably indicates that people generally would have understood that this is the way parent/child relationships should be conducted. But, given that Paul goes on to use Scripture to make his point, it may be that he is referring to what is right in terms of God's will for Spirit-filled children. Children, like adults, are to *find out what pleases the Lord* (5:10), and this obedience to parents is **right** in that context. Interestingly, in a similar passage in Colossians 3:20, Paul actually says: 'Children, obey your parents in everything, for this pleases the Lord.'[1]

The word used for obeying here is often used by Paul of obedience to the Lord himself and to the gospel. For example in 2 Thessalonians 1:8: 'He will punish those who do not know God and do not *obey* the gospel of our Lord Jesus.' And it is this that is highlighted by the phrase **in the Lord**. These children have a relationship in their own right with the Lord. They are first responsible to him and, because of their relationship to the Lord, they will desire to obey their parents, thus obeying the Lord. This is because it is the Lord's clear instruction, says Paul, quoting the fifth commandment: **Honour your father and mother** (Exod. 20:12).

This command is now expounded in an attractive and non-threatening manner. It has a **promise** attached, **that it may go well with you and that you may enjoy long life on the earth**.[2] In its original context in Exodus 20 this long life would have referred to living in and enjoying the privileges of the Promised Land of Canaan. Paul now generalises from that original promise as he speaks to Jew and Gentile converts. Obedience to God's law is indeed likely to lead to a quiet, peaceable and

---

1 See also 1 Timothy 5:4.

2 *that it may go well with you* is not found in the Hebrew of Exodus 20:12, but it is found in the Greek version of the Old Testament, the LXX.

stable life and, hence, one that is normally likely to be lengthy. Of course, there will always be exceptions to this, just as there were to the promise in the Old Testament. But Scriptures do teach that following the will of the Lord will lead to a better and more enjoyable life generally, and this point is made specifically to children by way of encouragement. A lot lies ahead for godly, Spirit-filled children and they should look forward to their lives walked **in the Lord** in anticipation of all that he has in store for them.

In terms of application, it is important to note that in both Jewish and Roman societies of that time, this sort of obedience would not only have referred to a younger child doing whatever his or her father wants. Both societies regarded honouring parents as involving older and grown children looking after their parents in their old age and caring for them. Paul himself makes this point in 1 Timothy 5:4:

> But if a widow has children or grandchildren, these should learn first of all to put their religion into practice by caring for their own family and so repaying their parents and grandparents, for this is pleasing to God.

In much of modern society growing up is about getting away from authority and parents. In biblical terms there is a sense in which this is true as husband and wife leave father and mother (Gen. 2:24), but this is never meant to leave parents uncared for, or dishonoured, or unrespected. The household relationships continue and do not suddenly come to an end simply because children have married and left home. While in most modern societies families do not all continue to live under the same roof, Christians do need to take note of the continuing obligation of children to their parents as they grow older.

ii) Instructions for fathers
In Roman law the father had rights over his children which would sound extraordinary to the modern ear, including the right of the magistrate even to put them to death in some circumstances. While many fathers would, no doubt, have

been loving and kind, nevertheless, the idea that a father should be given limitations on how to deal with his own children would have caused surprise. The Judaism of that period heavily stressed discipline and the father's authority over his children, but was also preoccupied with ensuring that the children grew up understanding their religion and its practices. The apostle says two things to fathers.

> Fathers, do not exasperate your children; instead, bring them up in the training and instruction of the Lord (6:4).

First, he wants fathers to treat their children with care. It is all too easy as a father to be so insistent on discipline in so many matters, some of which are likely to be minor and insignificant, that they can **exasperate** their children who can then end up becoming exceedingly frustrated. The Greek word is really stronger here, implying that children might become *angry*. Paul's point is that fathers, too, have to find what is pleasing to the Lord and walk a life that is Spirit-filled. In the Christian family where a relationship of authority and submission exists between father and child, there is still a way for the father to show in his family and to those around a new way of living. He is still governed, even though he has a God-given authority in the family, by the command to mutual submission in 5:21. These two things need not be opposed to each other. The father's submission will be seen in the way he shows he is *humble and gentle, patient* and *bearing with* his child *in love* (4:2). Such a father will not cause his child to become *angry*.

These commands in 4:2 and 5:21 were not surrounded by caveats such as 'except fathers when disciplining their children', or 'except husbands when dealing with their wives', or 'except masters when dealing with slaves'. As we have seen, Paul is showing how these commands can still be lived out even when people are involved in relationships which involve authority structures. The household structure and relationship is not done away with, but the commands affect how both parties will respect and work with each other.

As a father is forbearing to his children in refusing to drive them so hard that they end up breaking God's law and becoming angry, so he actually helps them **obey** their **parents in the Lord**. This leads to the other command to fathers.

Secondly, Paul wants fathers to teach their children about the Lord. In the Christian faith and as part of the body of Christ, fathers have a particular motivation for the discipline and care of their children and it is to **bring them up in the training and instruction of the Lord**. Their authority and headship in the family is most specially to be seen in how they point the family to the Lord and, with children, enable them to grow up knowing and loving him. This **training and instruction** will include teaching children what the Lord expects of a child who is Spirit-filled. It will include helping a child know Scriptures so that he or she is aware of how to find out *what pleases the Lord*. Because Paul has been talking about walking a *wise* life, this training will not just be theoretical about God and about Jesus but will be deeply practical about day-to-day life, as well as encouraging the child to look to the Lord in all things.

In this day and age it is often the wife who will teach the children about the Lord and there is nothing wrong with that happening, but it is good for the husband to realise that here, as father, he is being given the specific responsibility of ensuring the children grow up knowing, loving and following **the Lord**.

f) Spirit-filled household relationships – slaves and masters (6:5-9)

Paul now moves to another household relationship, that of slaves and masters and, as before, he begins with the one who has the subordinate role.

i) Instructions for slaves

In a church where slaves and masters from the same family were meeting as equals before God to worship, many must have questioned how this relationship was supposed to work in the household. It is easy to imagine the problems of class, social background, education level, and so on, all giving rise to interesting debates and discussions among members of the church. As before, though, Paul sees a way through which maintains the roles of slave and master, and the position of one with authority over the other, and yet upholds the principle of mutual submission in the Christian church.

> Slaves, obey your earthly masters with respect and fear, and with sincerity of heart, just as you would obey Christ. Obey them not only to win their favour when their eye is on you, but like slaves of Christ, doing the will of God from your heart. Serve wholeheartedly, as if you were serving the Lord, not men, because you know that the Lord will reward everyone for whatever good he does, whether he is slave or free (6:5-8).

As with the previous relationships, the motivation for slaves is ultimately to be their relationship with Jesus. They are part of the one body of Christ along with their masters in these Christian households, and so their service of the household takes on a completely new perspective. They too will be seeking to *find out what the will of the Lord is* (5:10) and so Paul says that obedience to the master (the Greek word is 'lord') will indeed be **doing the will of the Lord**. Slaves who are filled with the Spirit and *walk wisely* will do this from their **heart**. It will not just be a chore, but a way in which they can bring honour to the Lord of lords. They will of course be motivated in normal human ways of desiring to **win** the **favour** of their masters, but slaves should compare the service of their masters with being **slaves of Christ**, and with **serving the Lord**. The service of the Lord, **not men**, is to be the driving force behind the way slaves behave with regard to their human masters. In that relationship slaves may gain little in terms of material reward. However, Paul points to the clear equality of both master and slave before the Lord as he reminds slaves that **the Lord will reward everyone for whatever good he does, whether he is slave or free**.

The triple emphasis on the **sincerity of heart, from your heart** and **wholeheartedly** (with good will) is a reminder of just how unnatural this response of slave to master was likely to be and yet, because of the relationship with the Lord, a new human relationship is now possible within the body of Christ. As in the other relationships, this can only be achieved when a person is Spirit-filled, for it will require a radical change of heart that only God himself can bring about.

The future **reward** from **the Lord** reminds us that the final Master is one who always rewards his people and will do so at the last day when he returns. Whatever the attitude of the master of the household, the Christian slave knows that he is serving Christ in his life and attitude of heart to his work. Even if he receives no human reward, he will receive one from the Lord in due course, and this Lord rewards not just the **free** but also the **slave**.

In all three of the relationships of the household to which Paul has referred, different members have different roles, some carry authority over others and some bring with them subordination. But Paul has also been showing throughout that, whatever those roles, Christians are to be submissive to each other and are all part of the same body of Christ without distinction. He has been showing that all are Spirit-filled and seeking to do the Lord's will without distinction before the Lord. Any social and hierarchical distinctions in households in this life will disappear before the Lord on the last day as he rewards people for the lives they have lived for him.

ii) Instructions for masters

This point about the disappearance of social and household distinctions and roles in the presence of the Lord is now spelled out for **masters** as the apostle describes what mutual submission will look like for the master in this relationship.

> And masters, treat your slaves in the same way. Do not threaten them, since you know that he who is both their Master and yours is in heaven, and there is no favouritism with him (6:9).

Two important theological considerations should guide masters in how they treat their slaves. First, even **masters** have a **Master**.[3] Secondly, the Master who **is in heaven** shows

no favouritism. A master of his own household was, more or less, not answerable to anyone. But this is not so for the Christian master who was (**in the same way** as his slave) to recognise he was serving the Lord in heaven before whom he too would be accountable one day. And the master should avoid pride or arrogance here because, before the Lord on that final day, his social status will count for nothing. There will be **no favouritism**.

The challenge to masters and slaves in these verses is truly remarkable. In the Roman world into which Paul was writing, masters had enormous power over their slaves and were often known for instilling fear through beatings or even selling off other members of the slave family in an attempt to keep a slave in his or her place and to stop them running away. The sort of relationship that Paul is mapping out for them as Christians is entirely different.

While Paul is not doing away with the whole institution of slavery, what he says certainly indicates that, for Christians, slaves are fully part of the church, are Spirit-filled, and have a Lord to serve who takes precedence over the human master. With this wholly redefined relationship of mutual respect under the one Lord of both master and slave, it is not much wonder that gradually Christians began to move away from slavery as an institution.[4]

Perhaps this relationship of master and slave, more than any other, reminds Christians that it is possible to serve the Lord and bring glory to him in whatever work we may be called to do in life. Sometimes, from a human point of view, things may appear impossibly harsh and unfair, and yet still we are to find out what pleases the Lord and what his will is, and walk wisely before him, while filled with his Spirit. We can know with wonderful confidence that we serve a Lord in heaven who watches over us and who will reward without favouritism or distinction on that last day.

---

3 Greek: 'lords' and 'Lord'.

4 Slavery is thus not at all like marriage. Slavery can be handled in a Christian manner that reflects the unity now found between master and slave 'in Christ', but it is not said to be a reflection of the relationship between God and his people. Slavery is not present in the creation account, whereas marriage is.

Just as a slave is told not to work simply **when** the master's **eye is on you**, so we need to know that we cannot and should not rely on the eyes of men and women for our motivation or reward. Rather we look to our Lord who will never let us down or fail in his promises to us.

6

Be strong in the Lord
(Ephesians 6:10-20)

As Paul draws his letter to a conclusion, he pulls together a number of themes from what he has written and appeals to the Ephesian Christians to remember the wider context in which they are called to serve the Lord. The body of Christ is involved in a battle against evil spiritual powers and must move forward in the Lord's power, recognising that he alone can give the resources for living the Spirit-filled life and walking wisely. The battle imagery draws on the Old Testament picture of the Lord (Yahweh) as a warrior king who goes out to fight for his people. Paul gives a number of commands to Christians which will enable them to withstand attacks by Satan and his powers.

a) The Lord's mighty power (6:10)

> Finally, be strong in the Lord and in his mighty power (6:10)

Paul began the letter by pouring out his praise and thanksgiving to God for all the joy of the inheritance that Christians have *in Christ*. Specially he prayed that the Ephesians would have their eyes opened to see the Lord's 'incomparably great power for us who believe. That power is like the working of his mighty strength, which he exerted in Christ when he raised him from the dead and seated him at his right hand in the heavenly realm' (1:19-20). It is this power that must be relied upon as Christians live in a world where the forces of evil are constantly trying to undermine their position and inheritance.

This power is not something that Christians are able to produce for themselves and from their own efforts. Rather it comes from God and is *for us who believe*. In 3:16 Paul had written, 'I pray that out of his glorious riches he may strengthen you with power through his Spirit in your inner being.' God's people have to learn to enjoy and benefit from the power that they have in Christ and are given for day-to-day life by the Spirit. They are not on their own, struggling to survive through to and make the grade for the final judgment day. Rather they are secure as they trust the Lord and his **mighty power** for their strength. The Spirit who strengthens them is, after all, the same Spirit who is also the guarantee of their inheritance and redemption (1:14).

b) The enemy (6:11-13)

> Put on the full armour of God so that you can take your stand against the devil's schemes. For our struggle is not against flesh and blood, but against the rulers, against the authorities, against the powers of this dark world and against the spiritual forces of evil in the heavenly realms. Therefore put on the full armour of God, so that when the day of evil comes, you may be able to stand your ground, and after you have done everything, to stand (6:10-13).

It is wonderful to know that the battle has in fact been won, for Christians *are* (already) *seated in the heaven realms in Christ Jesus*. Nevertheless the victory must be appropriated by believers living in these times before Christ finally returns to rule, and so they are to **stand**.

It is essential that the church be aware of how real this battle remains and so in these three verses Paul describes the enemy and talks of the armour that is needed. The enemy is identified as **the devil**, and it is his **schemes** (trickery) against which God's people must battle. This deceit, cunning and scheming of the devil is the same as Adam and Eve experienced in the Garden of Eden (Genesis 3). It is constantly aimed at undermining the authority and rule of God himself and of leading people into sin and rebellion. But Christians belong to God and he has not only guaranteed the result of the battle, he gives them armour that can withstand the ongoing skirmishes and daily attacks of the Devil.

In 4:27 Paul pointed to the danger of giving *the devil a foothold*. Terms already used of darkness (4:18, 5:11) are now used to describe the enemy in more detail. It will be all too easy to give a foothold to an unrecognised enemy. Thus the battle is **against the rulers, against the authorities, against the powers of this dark world**. For this reason it is a **struggle** that **is not against flesh and blood**. Too frequently, Christians assume that various 'little' sins are not that important. Specially when it comes to life in the body of Christ, falling out with others, or parting from them because of some disagreement, or not treating them with the love, patience and forbearing of which Paul has talked earlier in the letter, these sins are often put down to the idiosyncrasies of particular individuals. Sin is excused or even taken for granted. Rather it is vital to know the tactics of the enemy and to see how he brings about division and deceit, for only then will sin be seen for what it really is in all its darkness. Such happenings are products of **this dark world** and are an attack by **the spiritual forces of evil in the heavenly realms**. They cannot be treated lightly or as insignificant.

The description of these forces, led by the Devil, as *spiritual forces of evil* again points to the fact that ultimately Christians are caught up in a battle between God and the Devil.[1] And yet, even though these forces continue to rule the realm of darkness, Christians now live in a different realm altogether. As we read in Colossians 1:13-14: God 'has rescued us from the dominion of darkness and brought us into the kingdom of the Son he loves, in whom we have redemption, the forgiveness of sins.'

As we shall see below, the armour we are given by the Lord is like the armour of God himself, and the **mighty power** with which we are enabled to fight is God's own power.

---

1 In Ephesus this battle would have been evident day by day as Christians lived in a society where the cult of Artemis dominated and magic and sorcery were a part of day-to-day life.

c) The armour (6:13-20)

This idea of 'putting on' the armour is very similar to what has been taught in chapter 4 where Christians were told to *put on the new self* (4:24). There we learned of the contrast between the works of darkness and the *righteousness and holiness* that Christians were to reflect as they were *created to be like God*. The reason for putting on this armour is so that **when the day of evil comes, you may be able to stand your ground**. These attacks by the spiritual forces are going to come in many different forms, so the church and individual Christians need to be prepared. **The day of evil** in this context seems to refer to particular times of attack and even persecution that Christians or the church will experience. There will be many such days when the church will feel under concerted attack and the temptation to give in will become acute. This is mirrored in the life of individual believers as well. There are the temptations to sin that come daily, but most Christians know there are those intense days, which they might describe as a 'day of evil', when the temptation is almost overpowering and the battle seems more intense than ever. Paul's concern is that Christians prepare in advance for such a day so that when it comes they may be able to *stand*.

The call to *stand* is repeated four times in verses 11, 13, and 14. The picture it evokes is of a soldier standing his ground against an on-coming enemy. He fights with his sword and other weapons at his disposal and refuses to give ground whatever the enemy throws at him. Some of the weaponry that this soldier of the Lord wears is now described.

> Stand firm then, with the belt of truth buckled around your waist, with the breastplate of righteousness in place, and with your feet fitted with the readiness that comes from the gospel of peace. In addition to all this, take up the shield of faith, with which you can extinguish all the flaming arrows of the evil one. Take the helmet of salvation and the sword of the Spirit, which is the word of God (6:14-17).

The picture is of a Roman soldier proudly and unswervingly standing his ground and using all the weapons, offensive and defensive, at his disposal.

i) *God's armour and the Old Testament*

Before looking at the individual items of clothing and weaponry, it is important to see how the apostle uses material that has its roots in the Old Testament and the description, specially in Isaiah, of God as the warrior King. For example, in Isaiah 42:13 we read:

> The LORD will march out like a mighty man, like a warrior he will stir up his zeal; with a shout he will raise the battle cry and will triumph over his enemies.

In Psalm 18 David calls upon the Lord to fight for him and also sees the Lord as enabling him to fight:

> The LORD is my rock, my fortress and my deliverer; my God is my rock, in whom I take refuge. He is my shield and the horn of my salvation, my stronghold (18:2).

> It is God who arms me with strength and makes my way perfect. He makes my feet like the feet of a deer; he enables me to stand on the heights. He trains my hands for battle; my arms can bend a bow of bronze. You give me your shield of victory, and your right hand sustains me (18:32-35).

In Isaiah 11 the prophet looks forward to the coming of the Messiah. This King will come to judge and will do so with the *Spirit of power* (11:2). Then we read in 11:4-5:

> He will strike the earth with the rod of his mouth; with the breath of his lips he will slay the wicked. Righteousness will be his belt and faithfulness the sash around his waist.

Isaiah 59:15-17 also provides obvious background for this passage in Ephesians:

> The LORD looked and was displeased that there was no justice.... he was appalled that there was no one to intervene; so his own arm worked salvation for him, and his own righteousness sustained him. He put on righteousness as his breastplate, and the helmet of salvation on his head; he

put on the garments of vengeance and wrapped himself in zeal as in a cloak.

As the apostle Paul builds on these various descriptions of God and the thoughts of King David and the prophet Isaiah in the Old Testament, we gain a very real sense that the armour and weapons that Christians have at their disposal are none other than the actual armour and weapons of God himself. Thus when Paul said in verse 11, **Put on the full armour of God**, while he may have meant the armour that God supplies, that comes from God, it is probable that he actually meant 'the armour that is God's own, that belongs to him and that he now shares with his people *in Christ*.'

ii) The belt of truth

The Roman soldier's **belt** was a leather garment worn round the waist that hung down to offer further protection for the thighs. It would have been one of the last pieces of clothing to be put on and would have been used to tuck in other parts of clothing to keep them from getting in the way in battle. Putting this on would have meant the soldier was ready for battle. **Truth** has been an often repeated theme in the epistle. Here, drawing on Isaiah 11:5, where the Messiah's belt is one of righteousness and faithfulness, the command is that the Christian should withstand the attacks of the enemy by continuing to act truthfully and with integrity (5:9). This involves a continuing commitment to *the word of truth, the gospel of salvation* (1:13).

iii) The breastplate of righteousness

The **breastplate** covered the chest and heart areas from sword attacks or from daggers, darts or arrows. Isaiah 59:17 lies behind this description: 'He put on righteousness as his breastplate.' In that passage God is seen to be clothed in his own righteousness and it is this **righteousness** which is to be put on by the Christian. It is part of *the new self*, the righteousness of justification. In the battle against evil powers, it is ultimately the fact that Christians can appeal to the righteousness of God as being theirs, that enables them to know they can withstand the attack fully and completely. However, the righteousness from God, which he imputes to the believer, must also lead to *acts* of righteousness. Thus part of the stand against evil will be countering falsehood with **truth**, and wickedness with **righteousness.**

iv) Well-shod feet

A soldier's shoes or boots needed to be properly fitted, to be flexible and tough. The Roman soldier used to wear a sort of half boot which enabled him to move quickly and to march long distances while still being well protected. Here Paul turns to another passage in Isaiah (52:7): 'How beautiful on the mountains are the feet of those who bring good news, who proclaim peace, who bring good tidings, who proclaim salvation, who say to Zion, "Your God reigns!"' The feet of Christians are to be prepared and ready (**fitted with the readiness**) with **the gospel of peace**. In Isaiah it is the Lord who brings peace, and those who proclaim the *good news* are proclaiming the Lord's rule (*Your God reigns!*). It is this method that Paul wants Christians to follow. Part of the way to defeat the Devil and his powers is both to rely for oneself on the fact that the Lord is all powerful and reigns, whatever the appearances may be to the contrary, but also to proclaim the victory of Christ to all who promote evil. The victory of Christ is above all to be seen in the gospel. He brings **peace** between Jew and Gentile and **peace** with God (2:14-17). Thus, there is a great irony here. One of the elements in being prepared for battle against the powers of this *dark world* is being ever ready to proclaim **the gospel of peace**, that is, to proclaim Christ as Lord of all.

v) The shield of faith

The shield that the Roman soldier used was large and protected most of the body. It was not dissimilar to the type of shield we sometimes see these days being held up for protection by riot police, except that it would have been made of wood and leather. This is an exceptionally important piece of armour which can be moved around and used for immediate protection from attack. Paul describes the shield of the Christians as **the**

shield of faith. As Satan attacks and tempts God's people, their need to rely entirely in faith upon the Lord alone becomes ever more vital to survival. Throughout history the church has seen those who have wonderfully modelled this faith in which the individual Christian is prepared to commit himself or herself entirely into the hands of the Lord and trust that he will deliver them whether in this life or the next. It is this sort of faith that has enabled Christians to suffer persecution even to their death for the Lord, but it is also this sort of faith which on a daily basis resists the attacks of Satan. This is what Paul means when he says, **with which you can extinguish all the flaming arrows of the evil one**.

The flaming arrows of the Devil's attacks will take many different forms. Some of his attacks will be designed to cause disunity among believers and to break up churches. Others will cause God's people to doubt God's promises. Some will attack the whole church and some will be more aimed at individuals and cause men and women to fall into the sin of greed or envy or immorality. As Paul speaks of this armour, his concern is that Christians realise the continuing nature of these attacks. It is no good to cope with one attack and then forget the **shield of faith**. This armour is to be the constant dress of all who are God's faithful people.

This letter has spoken of faith a number of times. Paul had expressed his thanks to God for the faith of these Christians in 1:15. He had reminded them that they were saved *by grace, through faith* in 2:8, and had prayed that Christ would dwell in their hearts *through faith* (3:17). Now it comes together at the end of the epistle. It is this faith that relies entirely upon the Lord and looks to him for help in the daily struggle with sin and temptation. It is this faith that knows he remains faithful to his people for ever that, in the end, enables God's people to **stand** and hold their **ground**.

vi) The helmet of salvation

Two further familiar parts of a soldier's armour complete the picture of the Christian and the church of Christ prepared for battle. The first is **the helmet of salvation**. Once again the picture is drawn from the description in Isaiah 59:17 of the

Lord himself as the warrior Lord: 'He put on righteousness as his breastplate, and the helmet of salvation on his head.' As Christians know, God himself brings about salvation and this is the point here. Paul moves from a list of characteristics that will enable the Christian to withstand the Devil, to something which now he or she must **take** or, more accurately from the Greek, *receive*. These last two elements of the armour are in effect saying, 'Make sure you take the greatest gift of all with you into battle! Go with the Lord himself!' God has won salvation for his people in Christ, and the Christian must receive this ultimate protection that is given by God to his people. In the ongoing skirmishes with Satan, God's people are to remember that they live under and for the Lord who is with them and has *already* won the battle.

There is an *already* and a *not yet* in this battle. *Already* salvation has been won by Christ as he died on the cross and was raised from the dead. This led to Paul being able to say in 2:6: 'And God raised us up with Christ and seated us with him in the heavenly realms in Christ Jesus.' We are already seated *with Christ*, and 2:5 – *by grace you have been saved* (past tense). Yet while the decisive battle has been won and salvation achieved by the Lord, we must receive it from him and take hold of it, recognising his saving presence with us, for the skirmishes and attacks that continue from the defeated foe until that day when Christ returns in glory.

At the time of attack and persecution and temptation, it is the fact that the Lord is our salvation that should be one of our greatest possible comforts as well as being one of our greatest weapons. We know the battle has been won and cannot be undone, and so we withstand the attacks and stand our ground because of what God has done in Christ. In Psalm 35:1-3, David expresses this great truth in a prayer that we may often have to make our own as we are attacked, tempted and persecuted:

Contend, O Lord, with those who contend with me; fight against those who fight against me. Take up shield and buckler; arise and come to my aid. Brandish spear and javelin against those who pursue me. Say to my soul, 'I am your salvation.'

The last piece of armour, which is also to be received as a gift from the Lord, is now mentioned.

vii) The sword of the Spirit

The sword of the Spirit which is the word of God is also to be received. A sword is not only a defensive weapon but one which can be used in attack, and part of the church's duty and that of individual Christians is to go on the attack against the Devil and the powers of this *dark world*. Once again it is God himself whom we are to receive here. It is he who has spoken. Isaiah 11:4 is probably in mind: 'He will strike the earth with the rod of his mouth; with the breath of his lips he will slay the wicked.' Just as God spoke and the world came into being in Genesis 1, so God speaks, or 'shouts' and his word prevails in battle. Thus we read in Isaiah 42:13: 'The LORD will march out like a mighty man, like a warrior he will stir up his zeal; with a shout he will raise the battle cry and will triumph over his enemies.'

What Christians therefore take with them is the proclamation of God's victorious word in the gospel. We are not always to be on the defensive, rather we go forward with the good news of Christ's victory raised high in our hands and shouted out to the world. Christ is King and Saviour, and his Word lasts forever and is fully mighty and effective in conquering Satan and his powers. We go forth with a proclamation of the victory won for us on the cross. We go forth with the Saviour himself (*with Christ*) and we proclaim *his* word and watch the power of the Spirit at work in the proclamation.

Both churches and individuals, who go forth with this sword and who are prepared to receive it and take it up for battle, are constantly amazed at how the powers of darkness recede. Nowhere is this seen more clearly than in the salvation of those who are gripped by darkness as they find that, by God's gracious gospel word, they can move from the kingdom of darkness to the kingdom of light. The great power of the Spirit in the extraordinary transforming word of God must never be forgotten by all of us who are engaged in the ongoing battle of this age. God has spoken and he continues to speak as his word is proclaimed.

Sometimes Christians forget the power of the Spirit and the word of God which brought them from darkness to light. They forget that the same power is still there and that the Lord still fights for his people. This is entirely a gift of the Lord and all of his grace. As the great hymn says:

> We rest on thee, our shield and our defender!
> We go not forth alone against the foe;
> Strong in Thy strength, safe in Thy keeping tender,
> We rest on Thee, and in Thy name we go.
> Yes, in Thy name, O Captain of salvation!
> In Thy dear name, all other names above,
> Jesus our Righteousness, our sure Foundation,
> Our Prince of glory and our King of love.

All who take up this spiritual warfare must be entirely dependent upon the Lord, and so a command to pray is to be expected.

d) Pray in the Spirit (6:18-19)
It is in prayer that, above all, the Christian shows his or her dependence upon the Lord who hears his people and cares for them and answers all their prayers in accordance with his perfect will.

> And pray in the Spirit on all occasions with all kinds of prayers and requests. With this in mind, be alert and always keep on praying for all the saints (6:18).

Prayer itself is not one of the weapons with which a Christian is to fight, rather it is the means by which Christians ask their Lord for the necessary armour. It is he who supplies the weapons and helps them in the fight. Since the fight is a spiritual fight, prayer **in the Spirit** is essential. This is not, as some have suggested, an ecstatic form of prayer or prayer in tongues. Rather in this sort of prayer the believer will be aroused, encouraged, directed and guided by the Holy Spirit. Christians have been *built together to become a dwelling in which God lives by his Spirit* (2:22) and so, as they get involved in the fight, they will turn to God the Holy Spirit who lives among them and with them. He alone knows exactly what Christians will need in the many different situations they will face in life, and so he enables them to pray to the Father, even when they are not sure how to pray (Rom. 8:26-27).

i) Pray on all occasions
The urgency and importance of this prayer is emphasised by the repeated use of the word **all**. Paul reminds his readers that a constant battle needs constant prayer. Paul himself has shown the Ephesians what he means by this in 1:16: 'I have not stopped giving thanks for you, remembering you in my prayers.' Sitting in prison, writing to those who are involved in the front-line battle with Satan in a town where many gods were worshipped, could have left Paul feeling helpless. Yet he knows what it is to depend on the Lord for his friends and for their spiritual survival. In Colossians 4:2 Paul urged the Christians, 'Devote yourselves to prayer, being watchful and thankful.' There is never a time when we should not be in touch with the one who has brought about our salvation and will continue to help us each day in facing the kingdom of darkness.

ii) Pray with all kinds of prayers
Different words are used here to accentuate the urgency of intercessory prayer. As Christians seek to fulfil the command to *stand firm* (6:14) they will have many requests for themselves and for each other. They may need to pray for peace, or comfort, or protection or to be delivered from temptation. They will also need to pray for the proclamation of the gospel and the advance of the word of God against the kingdom of darkness.

Just as the attacks will be constant so the church's prayers will continue to rise to the one who alone can and does save.

iii) Pray with all perseverance
Hand in hand with praying **in the Spirit** is being **alert**. Just as an army on a battlefield will never relax its guard, neither will the church. They are to be **alert** for the attack and one of the

signs of being alert will be that they **keep on praying** (Greek: *with all perseverance*).

iv) Pray for all the saints
Specifically the prayers are **for all the saints,** that is, for each other, for the church and for those Christians around us, and even for those we do not know but who fight the same battle against Satan. It is easy to get too caught up with our own battles, and to become too introspective and preoccupied with ourselves. And this verse reminds us that, as Paul prayed for Christians many miles away facing many diverse problems, so we are to pray **for all the saints** and that will include praying for some who are facing far worse battles than we shall know. The battle is continuous and world-wide. In Christ the victory has been won but we continue to face the enemy who seeks at all times to undermine those who worship Christ. For this reason we must see intercessory prayer, prayed **in the Spirit,** as the vital means to achieve the Lord's own victorious ends and our own protection, and so we shall *stand.*

e) The ambassador in chains (6:19-20)
Paul's thoughts have turned to salvation and to the gospel, the word of God (v. 17). He has called for urgent and continual prayer for all the saints and so he thinks of his own calling and his own needs. He prays for the Ephesians regularly, but he too needs prayer that the armour of God will protect him and help him fight the battle.

> Pray also for me, that whenever I open my mouth, words may be given me so that I will fearlessly make known the mystery of the gospel, for which I am an ambassador in chains. Pray that I may declare it fearlessly, as I should (6:19-20).

Paul's calling is to proclaim the gospel. His work requires taking *the helmet of salvation and the sword of the Spirit, which is the word of God* and going into battle. We have already seen, as we looked at 3:3-6, why Paul refers to the **mystery of the gospel**. The mystery has been revealed in Christ and that revelation is the revelation of salvation for people from all over the world who turn to Christ in faith. Paul uses the language of international diplomacy. Just as an ambassador represents the King or President of his or her country in the presence of another country, so Paul sees himself even in prison as one who, though working in the *dark world*, nevertheless stands in the place of and represents his King, Jesus Christ. It would be all too easy to find the imprisonment an excuse for no longer proclaiming the gospel. Twice Paul prays that he may speak **fearlessly**. This is what he needs prayer for. He, like so many persecuted Christians through the ages, probably faced daily the attacks of the Devil that tempted him to stand back from the fight or to keep quiet about his faith. He begs for prayer that he may **declare** the gospel fearlessly, for this is what he **should** be doing.

The apostle also asks for prayer that he may be given by God the right **words** to speak so that the gospel will be heard and understood. So intent on communicating the gospel is he that he asks that he be given these words **whenever** he opens his mouth. In this last appeal for prayer Paul shows that he too is as dependent upon the Lord as anyone to whom he writes. It is only by God's grace and God's provision that the gospel will be heard and received and people come to faith. And it is only by grace that Paul can fulfil his calling to speak.

It is likely that 2 Timothy 4, describing the last days of Paul's life on earth, spells out the result of this prayer for him. Even while imprisoned in Rome he continued to take every occasion to speak the gospel. In the presence of another king, Caesar, Paul stands for the King of kings and proclaims Christ's victory on the cross and his resurrection and Lordship. It was not easy to do this. His friends had left him to face trial on his own. The question he faced was would he indeed **fearlessly make known the mystery of the gospel**? Or would the attacks of the evil one stop him fulfilling his calling? And so he writes:

At my first defence, no one came to my support, but everyone deserted me. May it not be held against them. But the Lord stood at my side and gave me strength, so that through me the message might be fully proclaimed and all the Gentiles might hear it. And I was delivered from the lion's mouth. The Lord will rescue me from every evil attack and will bring me safely to his heavenly kingdom. To him be glory for ever and ever. Amen (2 Tim. 4:16-18).

Further Application

First, we should note the importance Paul gives to prayer. It is perhaps one of the strangest anomalies of the modern church that while it often spends much time talking of how evil the world is and how dreadful society has become, the same church spends little or no time in prayer. This letter has shown us Paul's personal commitment to prayer for this church, but in these last verses Paul has shown how vital the prayer of the congregation is as it battles the spiritual forces of evil. It seems so very sad that many churches and many Christians see little need for corporate, intercessory prayer. Some Christians do spend time in their own personal prayers, but often these tend to be simple prayers asking God for this or that. Such prayers are important, but they should not be allowed to become more important or given more priority than those prayers about the big issues, about how we live for Christ, about how we resist evil and fight the fight the Lord has commanded.

If this is true at the personal level, it is also true at the congregational level. How few people treat congregational or whole church prayer as a necessity. Yet we are to 'be alert and always keep on praying for all the saints'. I have been in countries where Christians have put themselves in great personal danger while gathering for prayer that they regard as essential to the church's survival. Why should such people treat prayer as so vital while congregations in Britain, the United States and across the western world so often ignore this indispensable Christian activity? The only cost to these people would be a little less time to eat dinner, coming home from work a little earlier, or a little less time with the family watching TV! The result of the lack of prayer is everywhere to be seen, for the spiritual forces of evil are at work in our midst. Consumerism, materialism, individualism and the other gods of our age seem to have influenced our Christian thinking far more deeply than we imagine. We shall only 'keep alert' properly when we pray together.

Secondly, we need to be careful not to give Satan too much power. Some Christians talk so much of the powers of darkness and the forces of evil and the power of the Devil that we might think Christ had never come and conquered! It is right and proper to realise, with these verses in Ephesians, that the forces set against God's people are of Satan and are dangerous. But we recognise this in the context of Christ's victory on the cross, and in the knowledge that we are God's people 'in Christ' and that Christ keeps us and guards us. We also know that we have been given the Holy Spirit 'who is a deposit guaranteeing our inheritance until the redemption of those who are God's possession'. Satan does not have enough power to undo the guarantee. His power is limited, even though the battle continues and is real.

More must be said, though. For there are other Christians who are indifferent to the works of evil around them. They do not feel the need to put on any armour, for they do not understand the battle and how they are being affected by the forces of evil. These people are in deep danger. Perseverance and being alert to the attacks of Satan and to the subtle ways he may influence us in our thinking and behaviour are essential if we are to grow in Christ. Underestimating Satan's attacks will be seen in our lack of attention to reading the Word of God, or our lack of commitment to individual and corporate prayer.

Closing remarks
(Ephesians 6:21-24)

Thus, Paul comes to the end of his letter. He has heard much about the Christians at Ephesus, as he indicated in 1:15. He prays for them regularly. He has spoken of the joys they share in being *in Christ*. He has talked of the great riches of the inheritance that is theirs *in Christ*. He has encouraged them to live together in the church in unity and in a way which reveals light rather than darkness. But Paul knows some of the Ephesians will be concerned for his imprisonment, specially now that he has asked for their prayers. They will want more details. And so he speaks to them of Tychicus who will be taking the letter to them:

> Tychicus, the dear brother and faithful servant in the Lord, will tell you everything, so that you also may know how I am and what I am doing. I am sending him to you for this very purpose, that you may know how we are, and that he may encourage you (6:21-22).

In Acts 20:4 we learn that Tychicus travelled with Paul on his third missionary journey and came from the province of Asia in modern day Turkey. He also delivered the letter to the Colossians, perhaps on the same trip that involved his journey to Ephesus, and is mentioned in much the same way at the end of that letter in Colossians 4:7. He was clearly a personal friend and confidant of the apostle and helped him in many ways, hence Paul calls him a **faithful servant in the Lord**. He served Paul but did so because this was his service to the Lord. And so, at Paul's request, he takes the letter to the Ephesians, but at the same time is asked to speak to the recipients and tell them more about Paul's personal details of his imprisonment and probably his health and state of mind. This would **encourage** them, because they would see how the Lord was looking after Paul even in the most adverse of circumstances.

> Peace to the brothers, and love with faith from God the Father and the Lord Jesus Christ. Grace to all who love our Lord Jesus Christ with an undying love (6:23-24).

Paul began his letter with a greeting in the style of a prayer that they would receive *grace* and *peace* from God, and here he ends with a similar prayer for them. **Brothers** refers to all the Christians in this church and, of course, includes sisters. **Peace**, as at the start of the letter, is a prayer that the Ephesians will continue to experience and enjoy the peace they have received through God's forgiveness when they were 'reconciled' to God. But as we have read the letter we see that this peace summarises Paul's concern for the unity of the body of Christ. So he is praying for their unity and peacefulness together in the gospel.

Paul then adds a prayer that they might know and enjoy **love with faith**. At the start of the letter he had commended them specifically with regard to their faith and love (1:15-16). But in the life of a church and in the lives of individual believers there is always further growth that is needed in both these God-given fruits of the Spirit. In a way Paul is simply summarising his longer prayer in 3:16-19. There he had prayed for the growth and development of understanding of love and faith: 'I pray that out of his glorious riches he may strengthen you with power through his Spirit in your inner being, so that Christ may dwell in your hearts through faith. And I pray that you, being rooted and established in love, may have power, together with all the saints, to grasp how wide and long and high and deep is the love of Christ...'

Peace, **love**, and **faith** come from both **God the Father and the Lord Jesus Christ**. The final sentence then sums up Paul's desire for this church with a prayer for **grace** for all who **love our Lord Jesus Christ**.

This whole letter has centred on God's grace. Paul rejoiced in God's saving grace in the opening chapters (1:7; 2:5, 8) and made it clear that the continuing service of the Lord needed his ongoing grace throughout the Christian life (3:2, 7; 4:7). The whole of life for those who **love** the Lord is a life lived in and through **grace,** and so this final sentence contains not just a traditional Christian benediction, but a genuine prayer that God's people will remain in and be sustained by the continuing grace of the Lord Jesus Christ. The last two Greek words are translated in the NIV as **with an undying love.** This implies that it is the believer's love that must be 'undying'. While this may be what Paul meant, it seems more likely that the words (literally: *with immortality*) should go with the word *grace*. Thus Paul ends by praying for **love with faith** and **grace with immortality**, that is, that these Christians may know God's grace and his gracious gift of eternal life that has begun in this age and will continue for ever.

Summary of Chapters 5–6
Chapter 5 continued with the commands to *walk* in a way which imitates God. Paul continues to spell out the danger of immorality, unwholesome talk and the deception of many who do not follow Christ. He insists on the contrast between light and darkness, between living as Christ's people and living as unbelievers. The key to this Christian life is the Holy Spirit with whom we must be filled. A community of Spirit-filled people will seek to submit to one another. Paul then outlined what this submission should look like in various different household relationships.

Chapter 6 reminded the Ephesian Christians that they are in the midst of a battle and that they need the Holy Spirit, the Word of God and the whole gospel message if they are to persevere and to stand firm. Prayer will be critical for the church as it witnesses to the Lord and proclaims the gospel message. Paul himself asks for continued prayer for this work.

However, the closing words to a joyful and challenging epistle bring us right back to where we started. They remind us that we are *in Christ* and that all that we have is by God's amazing grace in Jesus Christ. We are to **love our Lord Jesus Christ** from the bottom of our hearts as we reflect on all that has been done for us and the nature of our wonderful inheritance in him. That love for the Lord will be reflected in our relationship of peace and love with others in the church as we witness to the kingdom of light. Our faith will remain steadfast as we rely on the Lord's gifts of the helmet of salvation and the sword of the Spirit, which is the word of God. As individual Christians, and indeed as the church, we will be fearless as we live and speak for our Lord Jesus Christ in the power of his Spirit. May God give us all the necessary grace, peace, love and faith truly to be the serving and witnessing church he desires.

Subject Index

Scripture Index